To Di...

John and Betty Stam

Rachel Lane

CF4·K

10 9 8 7 6 5 4 3 2 1

Copyright © 2020 Rachel Lane
Paperback ISBN: 978-1-5271-0530-0
epub ISBN: 978-1-5271-0601-7
mobi ISBN: 978-1-5271-0602-4

Published by Christian Focus Publications,
Geanies House, Fearn, Tain, Ross-shire,
IV20 1TW, Scotland, U.K.
www.christianfocus.com;
email: info@christianfocus.com

Cover design by Daniel van Straaten
Cover illustration by Daniel van Straaten
Printed and bound by Nørhaven, Denmark

Unless otherwise stated, Scripture quotations are taken from the HOLY BIBLE, NEW INTERNATIONAL VERSION®, NIV® Copyright © 1973, 1978, 1984, 2011 by Biblica, Inc.™ Used by permission. All rights reserved worldwide.

Scripture quotations from the King James Version are marked with "KJV".

All rights reserved. No part of this publication may be reproduced, stored in a retrieval system, or transmitted, in any form, by any means, electronic, mechanical, photocopying, recording or otherwise without the prior permission of the publisher or a licence permitting restricted copying. In the U.K. such licences are issued by the Copyright Licensing Agency, 4 Battlebridge Lane, London, SE1 2HX. www.cla.co.uk

To Die is Gain

Contents

The Day the Soldiers Came 7
A Voyage of Discovery 17
An Independent Spirit 23
Living by Faith 33
Missionary Child... 43
Standing on the Rock 49
Testing the Waters 57
Go Forward! 65
To China at Last 75
Blessings and Trials 87
Learning the Language 97
New Horizons 105
The New Mr. and Mrs. Stam 113
Becoming Parents 125
To Live is Christ ... to Die is Gain 135
A Miraculous Rescue 143
Triumph 149
China and the China Inland Mission 157
Hudson Taylor and the China Inland Mission 161
Communism in China 165
John & Betty Stam: Timeline 168
Thinking Further Topics 171

For Lex, Sophie-Rose & Beth

The Day the Soldiers Came

"Things are always happening otherwise than one expects ... the Lord helps us to be quite satisfied, whatever he sends our way this day," said John Stam in a letter to a friend, December 5th, 1934; the day before his arrest.[1]

It was just after eight in the morning when the first knock came. Breakfast already eaten and cleared away, Betty was with the Chinese maid (or "amah"), preparing baby Helen for her bath. Her husband, John, was settling down to a morning of letter writing and study, while the cook, Li Ming-Chin, was busy in the kitchen. The urgent thumping at the door, at this early hour, took everyone by surprise.

The man at the door was a stranger to John. "The magistrate told me to come," he explained, breathlessly. John could see that the man was agitated, his eyes large and frightened, the sweat forming beads upon his forehead. "The communist soldiers ... they were

---

1. Geraldine Taylor, *The Triumph of John & Betty Stam* (Chicago: Moody, 1935), p.100.

To Die is Gain

at Yang Chi last night. It's only fifty or sixty "li" away! You must be careful ... and you must be ready to leave at any moment."

A "li" was roughly equal to one third of a mile, and the soldiers would be on foot. John was not immediately concerned. There had always been risks to the missionaries settling here in Tsingteh, but they had been carefully evaluated before the decision had been made. The local magistrates had assured John that a Communist attack was unlikely; and should such a thing come to pass, the Government troops were close by to step in. They promised to protect the family – and that was good enough for John and Betty Stam, as well as the officials at the China Inland Mission, the organization that had sent them out. After all, being a missionary to China in the 1930s was never going to be free of risk. The Stams accepted that, and they trusted that God was in control.

So John was able to reassure the man at his door that morning. Smiling, he reached out to pat the messenger's shoulder.

"Don't be alarmed," he said, gently. "Thank you for coming to tell us. But I doubt they will come to this little place."

As the messenger hurriedly departed, John turned to find the cook close behind him, anxiety written all over his face.

"I think you should go," Li urged his master. "The Reds aren't like the local bandits. There are so many of them, they won't be afraid of a few Government soldiers. And they're so unpredictable – you never know where they will be next. They're here today and there tomorrow!"

Despite the man's insistence, John didn't want to react too hastily. His temperament was a calm, steady one, not given to impulsive decisions.

"We'll wait and see," he responded. "A pastor from the next province is due to visit this afternoon ... let's see what news he brings."

But in spite of John's optimism, things were to move much faster than that. A little over an hour later, a man was seen running down the main street of Tsingteh, panting and shouting.

"Hurry! The Reds are coming! They will soon be here!"

The magistrate had sent this man out into the countryside as a scout, to see if the rumors were true. It was confirmed: the Communist soldiers were now just ten li away. It would not be long. Upon receiving this alarming report, Magistrate Peng gave the order that the city gates be closed at once.

At the doorway of the Stams' house, Li looked out to see people running in all directions. With a mounting fear, he called desperately to John.

"Look! The Red soldiers must be near!"

John was surprised.

"Surely they couldn't travel so far in one night," he wondered, aloud. "But I'll go myself and see what I can find out."

To Die is Gain

As the door closed behind him, the maid Mei Tsong-fuh was seized with terror and began to tremble. She ran back into the room where her mistress was still tending to the baby.

"You need to finish quickly!" she exclaimed. "We must leave!"

Betty was aware of the growing danger, but her faith in God gave her an unshakable peace and, like her husband, she sought to offer comfort to the frightened servant.

"Don't be afraid, Mei," she said quietly. "We trust in God. There is nothing to fear."

Shortly afterwards, John returned with a conflicting report. The man he had spoken to claimed the Reds were actually much further away; in Chiki, seventy li south of Tsingteh. Li was incredulous – his own mother had witnessed the terrified Scout running back into the town, and he didn't believe this second report for a moment.

"Please, Mr. Stam!" he urged, frantic. "Let me go and order chairs and carriers for us, if I still can!"

John agreed that the cook could go, and went to find Betty.

"Why don't you get some of our things together in a bundle – just in case we do have to leave here for a few days," he suggested to his wife. "I'll do the same in the kitchen."

Hardly had he finished speaking when there was another insistent knock at the door. This time, a uniformed soldier sent from the magistrate.

"You must leave," he told John, firmly. "The Red soldiers will soon be in the city."

John nodded. It could no longer be doubted.

"Thank you," he replied. "We're just getting our things together now, and will leave as soon as possible."

Li returned, having managed to enlist the help of two carriers (or "coolies"). They agreed to transport the Stams and their belongings, and John accepted the price they proposed.

"The west gate is still open, we can get out that way," the coolies said. "The Red soldiers are coming from the east. But we need to go and look for chairs. All the chairs at the station were already hired."

"Then go!" Li exclaimed, his voice betraying his frustration and fear. "Go at once and find chairs!"

But at that moment, a burst of gunshots rang out from the direction of the city wall. John and Li exchanged glances; all but one of the coolies fled. It was too late.

Together, John and Li barred the doors of the house. Then, at John's bidding, the whole family, including the servants, knelt down together in prayer.

The cook had been right in his prediction, for the Red soldiers overpowered the local militia all too easily. What chance did less than a hundred men have against more than two thousand? With defeat inevitable, the magistrate disguised himself as a farmer and managed to escape the city. However, once the Red soldiers had scaled the wall and thrown open the east gate, the

To Die is Gain

entire force could enter easily and soon had the whole town surrounded. No further escape routes remained.

The missionary house was not far from the east gate. When the soldiers came, they soon broke through the door to the outer courtyard and proceeded to the main door to do likewise.

However, John decided to pre-empt them. Knowing that their entrance was inevitable either way, he and Betty opened the door and let them in. Four soldiers, perhaps in their early twenties, dressed in grey uniforms, with the red star shaped badge upon their caps. Each one armed with a rifle.

John saw four tired, damaged young men. He bowed and spoke gently to them.

"You have been through much hardship. What are your names?"

The soldiers' surprise was obvious, and they shared their names quite politely.

"You're a foreigner, aren't you?" asked one of the soldiers, an officer.

"I am an American," John replied.

"Do you have any medicine?"

John confirmed that they had some ointment, and gave it to the man. Looking around the room, the officer asked what else they had to give them. John willingly handed them all the objects of value he could think of, including a clock and a watch, a torch and a camera. As John fetched these things, at gunpoint, his wife boldly stepped forward and spoke to the other soldiers.

John & Betty Stam

"You must all be thirsty. Let me get you some tea and cake."

With their permission, she retreated to the kitchen and soon returned with refreshments for the weary men, who devoured them gladly. But the Stams' kindness couldn't long delay the inevitable: these were not men who had been trained to show mercy. The officer's mood soon deteriorated once the subject of money arose.

John handed them all the currency they had in the house, which was only between forty and fifty dollars.

"Don't you have more?" the officer demanded.

"No, I don't," answered John, truthfully. "We have only just come here to Tsingteh. We are here to serve God. Any money we have comes from Shanghai, a month at a time. This is all we have."

The officer's eyes narrowed.

"Search him!" he ordered, furiously.

Rough hands seized John, to the silent distress of Betty and the servants, but a thorough searching produced nothing more.

"Now you can come with me," the officer announced. "I will take you to the yamen[2] to speak with my leader. Don't worry," he added, his voice taking on an edge of sarcasm. "There's nothing to be afraid of. You'll have a nice time, and then you can come back home again."

---

2. A *yamen* is the headquarters or residence of a Chinese government official.

To Die is Gain

Before they took him, the soldiers allowed John and Betty to pray together once more before the small gathering. As he was led away, John instructed the cook to take care of his wife and child.

Once the four soldiers had taken John, other soldiers quickly flooded in and began to seize and bundle up anything they thought they could use.

"Where is the foreign woman?" one demanded of the servants, Li and Mei.

Li bravely tried to reason with them.

"Why do you need to take her? You have her husband. Have a little virtue; she is a woman, a woman who has just given birth to a baby three months ago."

But the soldiers pointed their rifles at the cook and snapped at him, "Who are you to tell us what to do? And why are you defending a foreigner? You're Chinese; this has nothing to do with you."

The soldiers called Betty from her room and she came out with baby Helen in her arms. Realizing they could not be dissuaded, Li continued to speak up for the family he had grown to love and deeply respect. "If you must take them both, then please don't separate Mrs. Stam from her husband," he pleaded.

The young amah, Mei, was unable to hold back her grief. She could not bear to be parted from her mistress and the sweet baby she had helped care for since her birth.

John & Betty Stam

"Please, please let me go with them!" she begged the soldiers, through her tears. They refused, and when she persisted, levelled their rifles at her.

"If you try to come with us, we will shoot you!"

Betty spoke kindly to her before they marched her away. "It's alright, Mei. It's better that you stay here and keep safe. Then if anything happens to us, you will be able to care for the baby."

China Inland Mission, Shanghai
Tsingteh, Anhwei.   Dec 6th, 1934

Dear Brethren,

My wife, baby and myself, are to-day in the hands of the Communists, in the city of Tsingteh. Their demand is twenty thousand dollars for our release.

All our possessions and stores are in their hands, but we praise God for peace in our hearts and a meal to-night. God grant you wisdom in what you do, and us fortitude, courage and peace of heart. He is able — and a wonderful Friend in such a time.

Things happened so quickly this a.m. They were in the city just a few hours after the ever-persistent rumors really became alarming, so that we could not prepare to leave in time. We were just too late.

The Lord bless and guide you, and as for us, may God be glorified whether by life or by death.

In Him,
John C. Stam[3]

---

3. Geraldine Taylor, *The Triumph of John & Betty Stam*, p. 102.

A Voyage of Discovery

More than forty years earlier, in the spring of 1890, a young man by the name of Peter Stam had sailed from Holland to the United States to seek his fortune. Tall and good-looking, with a sparkle in his eyes and an outgoing personality, there was every reason to expect that this young Dutchman had a bright future ahead of him in the U.S. But before he could get very far along the path of self-advancement, Peter's life took an unexpected turn.

"Here, Peter, I have something for you."

Margaret Neighmond was a devout Christian whom Peter had met soon after his arrival in America. Eager to improve his English, he gladly accepted the New Testament she offered him, which was printed in both Dutch and English. But if language learning was Peter's primary objective, Margaret had quite another in mind.

"Lord, please work in Peter's heart as he reads your Word," she prayed silently, as the young man went on his way. "Please would he come to know Jesus through it."

To Die is Gain

Peter began to study his new book diligently and it wasn't long before he began to be affected by the truths it contained. The book told him that he was a sinner. At first, Peter was taken aback by that, and he rejected the idea. Then, gradually, he began to look back upon his life in a new way, and he began to see that he had lived it completely for himself, without giving much thought to God or anyone else. "Yes," he realized, "I am a sinner."

Thankfully, the book also contained good news for sinners! Peter read with dawning joy the verse that would change his life – John 3:16. "For God so loved the world that he gave his only begotten Son, that whosoever believeth in him should not perish, but have everlasting life."

"'God so loved the world' – well, that surely includes me then," Peter mused, "' ... that whosoever believes should have eternal life' ... that means me, too!"

Once he understood what Jesus had done for him, Peter lost no time in asking God to forgive him, and to change his life.

"Lord God, I believe your Word and I want to accept Christ as my personal Savior," he prayed. "I surrender my life to the one who died for me. Give me the grace to live for others, to love others as you have loved me."

Peter still needed to find work and make a living in this new country he wished to settle in. But along with that, God enlarged his vision and added greater ambitions. He began to seek ways to reach out to people with the good news that had transformed his own life.

Peter moved to Paterson, New Jersey, where he met and soon fell for a young lady called Amelia Williams. As well as being a fellow immigrant from Holland, more importantly Amelia shared his committed faith in Jesus Christ. They married and began to raise a family together, as Peter also started work as a builder and contractor. He had been given some money by his father and was able to borrow some more in order to purchase some land on which to build houses, as well as the building supplies he needed to start a business. It wasn't long before the quality of Peter's workmanship, combined with his honesty and integrity, began to earn him a good reputation. He was hired to build many new homes in the suburbs of Paterson and over time his business expanded in other directions.

Despite the busyness of his working life, Peter made sure he was always there for Amelia and their growing family, which eventually included six sons and three daughters, although sadly one did not survive infancy. Peter and Amelia placed a high priority on the spiritual training and instruction of their children. Every meal time, three times a day when the table was laid, a Bible was placed beside each person's plate. Before any food was eaten, the family would pray and then read a chapter of Scripture. As soon as each child was able they would take their turn reading aloud around the

To Die is Gain

table, a few verses each. This sent a clear message to the Stam children as they were growing up – the things of God took first place in their home.

It was a strict upbringing, but a loving one. Certain things were forbidden: going to the theatre, dancing, smoking. They weren't even allowed a radio in their home (of course this was long before the age of television, let alone games consoles or smart phones!). However, other things replaced these forms of entertainment; not only Bible reading and family worship, but books and music. Peter paid for all the children to have music lessons and as they grew in proficiency a family orchestra was formed and many a happy evening was spent playing and singing together.

However, although Peter and his wife tried to guard their children from worldly influences at home, they did not grow up unaware of the darker side of life. In fact, the children came into contact with many troubled people through the "Star of Hope" mission that Peter had founded in order to reach out to the needy in Paterson, both with material help and also with the gospel.

Ever since he himself was converted, Peter had been eager to communicate the good news about Jesus with others. Even during their early married life, when he had been busy building up his business, Peter had also been building up a team of people to engage in mission to the local community, especially the underprivileged. Recruiting volunteers from several of the town's

John & Betty Stam

churches, he formed a team who would visit prisons, hospitals and homes for the elderly, telling people about Jesus. Peter also went to taverns (or bars), into factories and workplaces, and out onto the street sharing the good news with all who were willing to listen.

As this outreach grew, so did the need for a base. At first they used a small local hall, but later they found they needed more space and began praying for somewhere else. Peter discovered a large unused stable in the heart of the town that he believed could be perfect for the mission. He was able to buy it and renovate it with the help of Christian supporters, and thus the "Star of Hope" mission was born. With a lot of hard work, the dusty old stable was turned into the ideal venue, with an auditorium that could seat six hundred people, as well as many other rooms that served as offices, classrooms and bedrooms for staff workers. The mission hosted regular evangelistic meetings and classes as well as sending more and more workers out. And over the next decades, many hundreds of people, from many different backgrounds and nationalities, would be led to Christ through their efforts.

For the Stam children growing up, the Star of Hope mission was a big part of their lives. Whether they were always conscious of it or not, they learned a great deal through what they witnessed there – about Christian service, but also about the hardships of life in the real world, and about grace and second chances. The family also went along to Paterson's Third Christian Reformed

To Die is Gain

Church, where Peter was not only an elder but also a committed Sunday school teacher. The children went to Sunday school every week as well as extra catechism classes on a Saturday, where they were drilled in the key doctrines of the Christian faith. During the week they attended the Christian Grammar school, where they also received biblical training and instruction.

So unlike his father, John Cornelius Stam, the fifth of the six sons born to Peter and Amelia, grew up surrounded by Christian teaching. However, the young boy was always aware that he would have to decide whether or not to accept the Christian faith for himself. No one tried to force him to make this decision, even though his parents and older siblings prayed that he would. It was clear from an early age that John, while being an obedient and industrious lad, possessed a strong independent streak. He would make his own mind up.

An Independent Spirit

At the end of a long, tiring day on her feet, Amelia Stam was glad to sit down and snatch a few quiet minutes to herself. Remembering John needed a button sewn on, she dutifully reached for her mending basket, but the shirt was gone.

"That's odd," she thought, knowing that she had put it in there earlier. Reluctantly pulling herself up from the chair, she went off to investigate, only to find John wearing the very shirt she was preparing to mend. The little boy beamed up at her.

"I did it myself, Mother!" he said, with a shrug. Having observed his mother do the job time after time, he had not found it difficult to fetch the needle and thread and simply copy what she did.

Amelia was surprised, but as the years went on she and Peter observed their son using his own initiative increasingly. He was strong and capable, and liked to do things for himself whenever he could. When there was a job to be done, a path to be laid, or a tree to be rooted up, John could always be relied upon to "pitch

To Die is Gain

in and do it"; often without assistance. It was a trait that his teachers also came to value. He was known to be reliable, hard-working and polite.

But when he graduated from the Grammar School, aged fourteen, John's independence showed itself again. Despite his father's offer to fund further education, he declined. Instead, he decided to pursue a career in business, and enrolled in training courses where he learned book-keeping and shorthand. Having still not accepted Jesus as his Savior, John was looking elsewhere for what might make him happy in life, and making some money seemed a good place to start.

It wasn't that John had definitely decided against being a Christian; far from it. He was still involved in all the church activities and was often to be found down at the mission hall, but he felt somewhat detached from the people he saw there. Many of those who came to the mission were "down and outs"; people with difficult backgrounds who had turned to drink and drugs or criminal activities. It was wonderful to hear their conversion stories and see how God had turned their lives around; but privately, John felt he had little in common with those people. He had always been to church; he had always lived a "good" life. Although he knew in his head that the Bible teaches that "all have sinned and fall short of the glory of God", in his heart he hadn't really accepted that he was just as much in need of God's forgiveness as those desperate people he saw at the mission.

John & Betty Stam

It was during the spring of 1922, the same year that John began his studies at Drake Business School, that things began to change. He was fifteen years old, but so tall and manly looking that he could easily have passed for twenty. Yet beneath the increasingly grown up, confident image that John projected to the world, inside he was uncertain and unhappy. Although he didn't realize it yet, a big part of this unhappiness was the Holy Spirit at work in him. We can never rejoice in the "good news" about Jesus unless we have truly believed the "bad news" about ourselves. John was being convicted of his sin.

In late May of that year, a blind evangelist named Thomas Houston came to give a special series of talks at the Star of Hope mission. On the Sunday evening, John was there, seated near the back of the auditorium with his younger brother Neil and one of his older brothers, Jake. Jake was a committed Christian who had been praying for his brothers for years. As the evangelist spoke, John had been increasingly convinced of the truth of his message. But he didn't feel he was completely ready to give his life to Christ; not yet.

It was common at the end of these meetings for the speaker to challenge people quite directly, which a private person like John found very awkward.

Sure enough, at the end of the meeting, Houston called upon all those who "were there without Christ" to stand up.

To Die is Gain

"Go ahead, don't be embarrassed," he urged them. "It's really important that you be honest with yourselves tonight about where you stand before God."

As a small number of people quietly rose to their feet, John stayed firmly in his seat. He wouldn't dream of drawing attention to himself like that — and have all those people, his brothers, mission workers, family friends and strangers, looking at him in surprise!

However, the evangelist's next invitation made him feel even more awkward. Having told those people to sit down again, he then asked all those who had accepted Jesus as their Savior to stand! John knew in his heart that this wasn't him; but as so many around him got to their feet, including his brothers, he was too embarrassed not to stand up with them. Surprised, Jake turned to his brother with a great big grin.

"Praise the Lord!" he said, hugging him. "Look, those who have accepted Christ tonight are all going down to the front." Gesturing to Neil also, he suggested, "Why don't you both go to the front and make your commitment public?"

John shook his head hastily and he and Neil slipped out of the meeting a few minutes early to make their way home. But Neil's change of heart was genuine. When the rest of the family returned home, he confided in Jake.

"John and I were both convicted of our sin and gave our lives to Christ tonight. We weren't brave enough to stand up at the front, but we have put our trust in Jesus as our Savior."

John & Betty Stam

Delighted, Jake prayed with both John and Neil, and later that night shared the happy news with the rest of the family. John said nothing; what could he say? If anyone noticed his quietness, they didn't comment. But inside, he was uncomfortable. He knew in his heart that he hadn't yet given his life to Jesus, despite what Neil had said.

The following day at college, John felt thoroughly miserable. Unable to concentrate on his work at all, instead he kept thinking about his own failings. He realized that while he wasn't living an openly sinful life, getting drunk or stealing like some of the people who came along to the mission, he was no better than them. He had thought that his church activities and respectable lifestyle made him good enough for God. Now he realized that wasn't true at all; he had been self-righteous and proud, and not only that, he had been deceitful, letting his family think he was a Christian when really he wasn't. If anyone needed a Savior, surely it was him!

So right there at his desk, John did what he needed to do: he prayed.

"Lord, I'm sorry for my foolishness and pride. Please forgive me. Thank you for sending the Lord Jesus to die on the cross for my sins. Please come into my life as my Savior and my Lord. Amen."

Even once John had become a Christian, he still inwardly squirmed at the prospect of any sort of

To Die is Gain

public ministry. The idea of being involved in any of the open-air meetings or door-to-door evangelism that volunteers from the mission engaged in scared him to death. What if someone from college saw him? They might laugh at him! So if he ever came across a group from the mission out in public, singing or preaching, John went out of his way to avoid them.

That summer, however, his faith was put to the test. Usually, the warmer months were a peak time for the mission's outdoor evangelism, with teams going out regularly to the streets and parks to share the good news. John began to notice that this wasn't happening this year, and it bothered him. Why were all these opportunities being wasted?

Eventually he was so concerned that he asked his father about it. "Why isn't the band out preaching?"

His father's reply was more than he had bargained for.

"It's up to you, John, to make a beginning."

"Me?!" John replied in astonishment. "Why me?"

His father smiled. "You're old enough now, John, and we have no one else to lead that part of the work this summer. Why not you?"

John was far from enthusiastic. But it was a wise decision of his father's, as it forced him to confront one of his biggest fears. John wanted the gospel message to be preached – he just didn't want to be the one to do it. However, once he began, he soon realized it wasn't nearly as difficult as he had thought. In fact, his fears

John & Betty Stam

about what other people thought began to melt away as he experienced the joy of telling others about his Savior. Along with his younger brother Neil, John spent many summer evenings out on the streets, witnessing for Christ.

The following year, John completed his studies at business school and over the next six years he worked in various offices in Paterson and New York. Capable and dependable, he earned a good reputation and was at the beginning of a promising career.

Working in the heart of New York City gave John a lot more experience of life and broadened his view of the world. His offices looked out onto the busy shipping yards, where vessels carrying passengers and freight came and went, to and from countries all over the world. It caught John's imagination as he tried to picture the distant shores and foreign cultures they might be travelling to. During his lunch breaks he often strolled around the streets, observing the contrasts of city life. On the one hand, there was Broadway and Fifth Avenue, the glitz and glamor, the lavish displays in department store windows. On the other, there was Chinatown and other downtown neighborhoods, where John saw poverty and squalor that appalled him. Everywhere, though, he saw people who desperately needed to hear about Jesus Christ.

As his faith was growing, John began to feel increasingly divided. Although he still helped at the

To Die is Gain

mission as much as he could, the bulk of his time and energy was inevitably spent on his work at the office. Yet when he had set out on this career path, he hadn't known Christ personally. Now that he did, the ambition to make money that had once driven him no longer satisfied. His heart was elsewhere. So, at the age of twenty-two, John decided to resign from his office and commit himself to full-time Christian ministry. His employer tried to dissuade him, wanting to keep hold of a promising and reliable employee. But John stood his ground, and left to work full-time at the Star of Hope mission.

He soon had a chance to really step up and prove himself there when his parents, Peter and Amelia, decided to take a trip back to their homeland of Holland. They felt confident in doing so, knowing that they could leave the mission in the hands of John and Neil while they were away. As it turned out, this was a harder challenge than John had envisaged. It wasn't the mission work so much as the task of managing people that he found difficult. Some disagreements arose between the workers at the mission and as John tried to deal with the situation he felt very young and inexperienced.

As he sat in the office one morning with his head in his hands, trying to pray about the situation, John was overcome by a wave of discouragement.

"I am the wrong man to have anything to do with overseeing this mission work," he said to himself, miserably. When he opened his eyes, John's attention suddenly landed on a plaque on the wall opposite him. On it was a verse from the Bible that said, "It is God that girdeth me with strength, and maketh my way perfect" (Psalm 18:32 KJV).

With relief, John remembered that he was not alone in this. He felt inadequate: but God was more than adequate. This firm reassurance enabled him to carry on and do the best he could to manage the mission faithfully during his parents' absence. Even so, it had taught him a valuable lesson; he definitely felt that he did need more training to prepare him for a life of full-time ministry. After praying about it for several weeks, John decided to move to Chicago in order to study at the Moody Bible Institute.

Living by Faith

"Everything goes like clockwork around Moody's," wrote one of John's brothers after visiting him there. "It has to, with such a crowd! And everything is early – breakfast at 7:00, lunch at 12:30, supper at 5:30, and meals are through in half an hour. Practically every student does some work ... and in such a happy spirit! Hymn singing bursts out all over the place, kitchens and washrooms included, all the time."

Another visitor observed, "Everywhere one feels that Jesus is in the midst and that the Bible is honored."

The buildings and equipment at Moody's Bible Institute were far from state-of-the-art; in fact they were rather old and outdated. Yet, the atmosphere John found there amongst its thousand or so students was warm and Christ-centred. The curriculum on the Missionary Course he had enrolled in was practical and wide-ranging, and John threw himself into his studies with his usual diligence. A year later he recognized a need for more intense study of the Scriptures, so he transferred into the General Bible Course. Hard-

To Die is Gain

working and amiable, it wasn't long before John had earned the respect both of his professors and his fellow students.

"He had the bearing and mind of a college or university trained man," remembered one faculty member later (this despite the fact that John had finished his formal education at fifteen). "He was a young man of arresting personality and unusual Christian character. He was well balanced and energetic, possessing good judgment and considerable initiative." John's experience helping at the Star of Hope mission had obviously equipped him well, for in his practical Christian work the same teacher described him as "a good speaker and an exceptionally good group leader."

Others also recognized something special in John. Another official at the college predicted: "He will undoubtedly be heard from." Yet another: "Expect to see this young man make good in a large way."

But despite excelling in his studies, John remained very down-to-earth and was well-liked by his fellow students. They saw his deep, committed faith and "passion for souls", and it inspired them; but they also encountered a friendly, gentle young man one could have fun with. "He was a regular fellow, if ever there was one," one of his classmates testified. John didn't put on airs or try to impress anyone with his piety. In fact, he was very humble, being only too aware of his own sin and weakness.

John & Betty Stam

"My only trouble is myself," he wrote honestly to one of his brothers.[1]

It was outside of the classroom, in fact, that John would learn some of his most valuable lessons during his college years. One of the first of these was just how much he needed daily time alone with God. The days were so long and full, not only with hours of classes and study but with countless group prayer meetings. Later things became even busier when John began working in the college dining room to help support himself financially, serving tables three times a day and eventually being put in charge of the kitchen! With so much going on it seemed almost impossible to find quiet time to read his Bible and to pray. Yet John soon realized that without it, everything else he did became mechanical and his spiritual life felt stale. So with considerable self-discipline he began to rise earlier each morning, at five o' clock, so that he could have a precious hour alone with God before the busyness of the day began.

Another crucial lesson John learned through his college years was that he could rely on God to provide whatever he needed. With parents who were comfortably well off, as well as having been in paid employment for several years, John had never before known what it was to be in financial need. Yet his savings were not enough to see him through his time at college. Of course, his parents could have helped, and certainly would have if they had realized his situation; but John

---

1. All quotations from *The Triumph*, p.18-19.

To Die is Gain

deliberately kept quiet. He knew that if he went into mission work, wherever he might end up, he would need to trust God to meet his needs, material and otherwise. Why not start right now?

So John did not share his needs with others, nor did he ask for any money. Instead, he began to take them to the Lord in prayer. On a practical level, he also worked hard to supply his own needs through his job in the college kitchens; but although this was time-consuming and strenuous, the pay was little. There were still many times when John found himself short of needed funds to pay his college bills. Yet somehow, when the date for payment rolled around, the money always seemed to be there. A five dollar bill, pushed into his pocket by a local minister. An envelope with his name on it, with a gift from an anonymous donor. On one occasion which John never forgot, a woman of meagre income sent him two dollars from the money she earned peddling things door to door – just like the poor widow Jesus commended in the Bible, who "gave out of her poverty". Sometimes the answers to John's prayers were humbling. Sometimes they made him feel downright uncomfortable ... like when a fellow student insisted on paying his school bill for that month.

"Roy, I couldn't take your money," John protested. "You'll need that to cover your own expenses later on."

"Well, I'll let God take care of that when the time comes," his friend answered, firmly. "I really feel that right now, He wants me to help you out."

John & Betty Stam

After some further hesitation on John's part, he eventually accepted the money. Particularly since his friend LeRoy insisted that if John didn't take it, he would simply pay the bill himself through the college mail system! Later, John reflected that it was probably good for his pride. "It has taught me what it means to be under obligation to others for my needs," he wrote in his journal that evening. "Some more self-sufficiency shattered!"

On another occasion, John was offered a lift home for the holidays by another student who was also from Paterson. It was a long journey, and the car would be very cold. John had no warm socks to wear, nor money to buy them. To make matters worse, a few days before they left John managed to rip one of the shirts he had planned to take home. He would mend it, but he knew his mother would notice and he didn't want her to know of his financial difficulties. As he went for a walk by the lake, John felt uncharacteristically gloomy. He found himself thinking:

"Well, it's all right to trust the Lord, but I wouldn't mind having a few dollars in my pocket!"

No sooner had this thought run through his mind than John kicked himself. As if the Lord wouldn't provide him with a million dollars if he needed it! Sure enough, just a few minutes later, as he was crossing Michigan Boulevard, John spotted a five dollar bill on the street. Soggy, but perfectly intact. "Oh, what a rebuke it was from the Lord! Just one of those gentle rebukes the Lord can so wonderfully give us."

To Die is Gain

The next day he went out and was able to buy two new shirts and a pair of good warm socks, just what he needed for the trip. Several years later he would write to a friend: "I am wearing those same socks still, and every time I pull them on, these cold nights, they preach a sermon on the Lord's wonderful power to provide, whatever my future needs may be."

When John first went off to study at Moody, he had no fixed plans for the future. He knew only that he wanted to follow wherever God might lead him. Many of the prayer meetings John attended at college opened his eyes to the need for overseas missionaries. He read prayer letters from far flung places in the world and found his heart deeply moved as he read of the countless multitudes who knew nothing of Christ. Who would tell them?

In the Stam family home there had always been a great deal of interest in foreign missions. Indeed, one of John's brothers, Harry, was already serving God in the Belgian Congo of Africa. So John was somewhat confused when his father didn't seem to support his own growing inclination towards overseas mission work.

Peter Stam reminded his son that "young people should not be swayed by merely human influences or personal desires in their choice of a lifework. And they should not overlook the need at home. I fear that sometimes speakers and missionary societies try to persuade young people, through emotions, to choose the foreign work."[2]

Peter's hesitation to give approval to John's plans lay partly in his own hopes for his son. As he himself grew older, he was well aware that a younger man was needed to take forward the work at the "Star of Hope" mission. He had privately thought that John would be the ideal man for that task, and hoped therefore that his son might return home to Paterson at the end of his time at college.

John felt torn. He wanted to honor his parents, so he weighed up their concerns carefully as he continued to pray about his future. But he still felt the call.

"The Lord knows where He wants me," he wrote to his brother Jacob, "whether in Holland, in Paterson, or some other place in the States, in China, or in India. However, it does look frightfully disproportionate to see so many here in comparison with the few over yonder. We know that the Lord's work is not overstaffed here, but, as someone has said, "There are those who simply cannot go and those who are free to go. Why should both stay at home for the same work?"[3]

One of the prayer meetings John attended regularly was for the China Inland Mission, a group that met each Monday evening in the home of Mr. and Mrs. Page, representatives of the mission in the south-west.

---

2. Vance Christie, *John & Betty Stam: Missionary Martyrs* (Christian Focus, 2008), p.49.
3. Ibid, p.49-50.

To Die is Gain

He often wrote to his father about the conditions in China, where Communist rebels were gaining ground and Christian missionaries were often in grave danger. Three missionaries with the CIM had already been killed, two others held captive. Understandably, Peter was greatly concerned about the prospect of John going out there himself.

"Why think of China or India?" he wrote to his son, "When there are other countries more open, would it not seem more in keeping with the Lord's will to go where work can be unhindered, rather than where life is always in danger and there is so much opposition?"

But God was at work. As John's burden for China increased, so his father's heart softened. Peter was utterly committed to the cause of the gospel. Could he try to hold back his son, who belonged after all to the Lord, and not to him? Peter and Amelia remembered how they had dedicated their son to God as a tiny baby, having him baptized before he was a month old. As they later testified, "We offered him, as we did all our other children, for the Lord's service as the Lord saw fit."[4] As the Lord saw fit. It was for him, and not Peter, to lay down the terms.

Eventually, Peter's letters began to reflect a change of heart on the matter of China.

"May the Lord richly bless you and guide you by the Holy Spirit to do His will. We must pray that more men may go to China."[5]

---

4. Ibid, p.26..
5. Ibid, p.50.

Something else significant was happening at those weekly prayer meetings for the China Inland Mission. At the same time that his commitment to missionary service was growing, John was beginning to find himself strangely attracted to another student who had her heart set on China. A quiet, gentle girl, already in her second year at Moody. Her name was Betty Scott.

Missionary Child

Dr. Scott was deep in thought at his study desk when he heard a gentle little knock at the door. A little knock he recognized.

"Come in!" he called, a touch sternly. The children knew that when he was in his study, their father needed to be left alone. But somehow it was impossible to be angry with Betty.

His eldest slipped quietly into the room, her round face lit up by radiant, dancing eyes.

"I'll go away again, I promise!" she exclaimed, skipping over to his desk. "I just want to tell you that I love you, Daddy!"

Contented by a quick hug and a kiss, the dark-haired little girl then scampered off to her play while her father watched her retreating form fondly.

Betty Scott thought herself quite the happiest of children, in surely one of the happiest of families. Her father and mother, Charles and Clara, were missionaries in the beautiful, coastal city of Tsingtao,

To Die is Gain

where they had moved just a few months after she was born. Four more babies had followed, two more daughters, Beatrice and Helen and then two little boys, Francis and Kenneth. Although Dr. and Mrs. Scott were kept busy with their missionary work, family life was very important to them, and they made sure their working pattern allowed for lots of time all together. Their family motto was "do it together" – and they did.

Every morning there were family prayers, with even the smallest taking their turn to pray and to choose which songs should be sung that day. Then, after a busy morning's work, Dr. Scott would always leave his study at eleven o'clock for a good hour of outdoor games with the children before lunch. They also enjoyed another precious hour all together each day before their early supper, when one of their parents would read aloud to them, from a whole variety of books.

The days were structured, but far from dull. The Scott children loved the security of their daily routine, but there was plenty of time for play, for freedom and discovery. They were outside almost constantly, exploring the woods and playing on the seashore. They didn't even have to go off to school in those early years, for an older cousin came to stay with the family and help with their education at home. Since there were no other children their own age to play with in the surrounding area, the brothers and sisters did everything together and a strong family spirit was forged. As the local church services were long and conducted in Chinese, their parents even led their weekly worship services at home each Sunday, teaching the children from the Bible in ways that were appropriate for their age and level of understanding.

Later Betty would always look back on those early years of her life as a precious blessing. She regarded them as having shaped her in a very significant way, as she explained in a poem she wrote for her father and mother as a young adult.

> *"Your loving courage never faltered,*
> *Your plans were gently laid aside,*
> *(That time my whole life-pattern altered)*
> *Obedient to our Lord and Guide.*
>
> *Imagine, in God's certain heaven,*
> *Your children made for ever glad,*
> *Praising the Lord for having given*
> *The dearest parents ever had."*[1]

Those happy years in Tsingtao eventually came to an end for Betty in her early teens, when she was sent to a boarding school in Tungchow, near Peking. It was a very great change for her, yet Betty took it in her stride. A cheerful and intelligent girl, she worked hard at her studies and soon made plenty of friends. One by one, her younger sisters and brothers followed her to the school and enjoyed the opportunities they had to be together. Even though sunny, gentle Betty was very popular with others her own age, she was

---
1. *The Triumph*, p. 31.

To Die is Gain

always motherly and kind towards her siblings. Many a Sunday afternoon was spent wandering around the campus together arm in arm with sister Helen, talking of home and school life, sharing secrets and memories. During these years, the whole family moved away from Tsingtao, but they still spent every Christmas together at the Scotts' new home in Tsinan, and the long summer months at a cottage by the sea in Peitaiho where they could swim, play tennis and read to their heart's content. Their father always had a lot of work to do, and the others helped when they were able by acting as his "secretaries".

Each of the children shared their parents' missionary heart. They had known and loved Jesus as their own Savior since they could remember, and they also dearly loved the country in which they had been brought up. Even though they knew they would need to go away for a time to study, all five expected to return to China as missionaries themselves; not because they had ever been urged to do so by their parents, but simply because it seemed to each the best way to invest their lives.

When Betty was seventeen, she was ready to go away to college in the United States – the most significant parting that the Scott family had faced up until that point. But it was also the year that the family were due a furlough – a long break from their missionary work to return home to the U.S. Knowing that their time all together was short, Charles and

Clara Scott had planned a special trip. The whole family were to spend six months travelling around the world together, visiting Egypt, the Holy Land, Greece, Italy, France and England.

The children were beyond excited as they packed for the months of travel and study that lay ahead of them. Each took a diary, which would be filled to bursting with notes and descriptions of the people and places they encountered upon their way. They were deeply moved by their visit to the Holy Land, thrilled to see with their own eyes the sites of many of the events in the gospel accounts of Jesus' life. They galloped on donkeys in Egypt, explored cathedrals and galleries in Venice and Rome, munched on Swiss chocolate as they climbed its glorious mountain paths. For Betty, it was a wonderful last chapter of her childhood, and left her full of excitement and anticipation for the future.

Traveller's Song by Betty Stam

I sought for beauty on the earth,
And found it everywhere I turned;
A precious stone from Singapore
That sapphire shone and sapphire burned —
A Rajah's ransom it was worth.

Eternal grandeur brooded deep
In Egypt's pyramids of stone;

To Die is Gain

And still I smell the orange bloom,
I see the frosty stars that shone
And cooled the tranquil Nile to sleep.

I loved the skies of Italy,
The swarthy, singing boatmen there,
The Virgins of the Renaissance,
With grave, sweet eyes and golden hair –
The land of Art and Melody.

Lingers long into the night
On snowy peaks the Alpine glow,
And every lake is loveliest,
And there, amid the endless snow,
I picked the edelweiss so white.

Before a Chinese city gate,
The entrance to an ancient town,
I saw the men fly dragon-kites;
While, by the willows weeping down,
Their wives beat clothes, from dawn till late.

Then home I came, as though on wings,
The joy of life in heart and eyes;
For, everything was glorified –
The earth, the ocean, and the skies,
And even all the common things.[2]

---

2. Ibid, p.33.

Standing on the Rock

"I'm afraid it's rheumatic fever," the doctor pronounced gravely, as he rose from Betty's bedside.

Betty's eyes met her mother's and read the anxiety written there, as the doctor explained that she must have full bed rest if she was to avoid permanent damage to her heart. Betty may have felt that she had arrived back from the world trip "on wings", but this unexpected turn of events brought her crashing down to earth. The plan had been for her to settle in the U.S. to study, but instead the next few months saw her flat on her back as the inflammatory rheumatism ran its course. Even once the worst was over, her heart was left so weakened that she was forced to remain in bed.

Still, there were blessings to be thankful for. The rest of the family were relieved that they hadn't returned to China sooner, so that in the event Betty had the tender care and support of her parents when she really needed it. It would also prove to be the time when Betty discovered her passion for writing. She had always loved words and been a great reader, but the enforced bed

To Die is Gain

rest gave her time and space to develop her literary skills. A deep thinker with a vivid imagination and a profound appreciation of beauty, Betty found in poetry the perfect outlet to express herself.

The months of illness changed Betty, teaching her patience in suffering. Her faith had been built on strong foundations in those childhood years, but now it was beginning to be tested. The Betty Scott who finally entered college in the fall of 1924 was quite different to the idealistic young girl she had been just a year earlier. She kept her sunny disposition and cheerful enthusiasm, but to this was added a depth of character and maturity beyond her eighteen years.

Inevitably, Betty's maturity and steady faith set her apart from others at college. Because she stayed away from parties where students smoked, drank and danced, some labelled her as "one of those religious people" and dismissed her. Yet Betty's warm, pleasant personality endeared her to most people over time, and once again, by the time Helen Scott joined her a couple of years later, she found that her elder sister was admired and well liked. She wrote:

> *"Betty had carved out real respect for herself on two scores — her literary gifts, which were admitted to be more than ordinary, and the depth and sincerity of her religious life. She was president of her literary society and editor of the literary publication, interested also in dramatics, and an active student volunteer. She was acknowledged*

to be one of the finest students in her class, graduating with a Magna Cum Laude. We were very close together at this time. Betty was interested in everything I went in for, especially athletics, which her heart condition would not let her take up, and she rejoiced in my little victories even more than I did."[1]

During the summer before her second year at Wilson college, Betty went to a Christian conference in New Jersey known as "Keswick", which was based on the English "Keswick Convention" that had been growing in popularity over recent years. It proved to be a very significant experience for Betty, stirring up her faith and inspiring her to dedicate her whole life to Christ afresh.

Her heart overflowing with joy, Betty wrote to her parents of the conference.

"Keswick" is over, but I trust never the message! Thank the Lord! I have now surrendered myself to the Lord more than I ever realized was possible. The Way is just Christ ... and complete consecration to his will in our lives.

I don't know what God has in store for me. I really am willing to be an old maid-missionary, or an old-maid anything else, all my life, if God wants me to. It's as clear as daylight to me that the only worthwhile life is one of unconditional surrender to God's will, and of living in his way, trusting his love and guidance.[2]

---

1. *The Triumph*, p.35.
2. Ibid, p.39.

To Die is Gain

After Keswick, Betty began to walk more closely with God day by day, learning to lift everything to Him in prayer and trusting Him more and more as she saw those prayers answered. She had felt God speak to her especially through Philippians 1 verse 21, which she took as her "life verse": "For to me, to live is Christ and to die is gain." She also began to pray earnestly about her future. "O God, if you so will, may nothing prevent me from returning someday to China as a missionary."

Once Betty had completed her studies at Wilson College, she enrolled at the Moody Bible Institute. She wanted to deepen her Bible knowledge, but she also knew she needed more practical experience of ministry. Much like her future husband, Betty was naturally a shy and reserved person and the idea of participating in things like prison ministry and street meetings was daunting initially. But she soon found great joy in telling others about the Lord she loved. It meant stepping out of her comfort zone, certainly; but to Betty, it was more than worth it. She expressed her deep awareness of the need to share the gospel in a poem she wrote at the end of her first year at Moody:

A Song of Sending

See, all the careless multitudes
Are passing by, now passing by,
The world is sick with sin and woe,
All men must die, some day must die.

John & Betty Stam

*The time set for our Lord's return
Is drawing nigh, draws ever nigh.
Send us in all Thy cleansing power —
Lord, here am I! Here, Lord, am I!*[3]

Just as Betty had impressed her fellow students and teachers at Wilson, so she did at Moody. It would have been very natural for someone like her to seem invisible among the large student body, with her quiet, gentle temperament and her unassuming appearance. She always dressed simply, without high heels or jewelry or any other touches of glamour. Her dark hair was usually parted on one side and fastened neatly in a low bun at the back of her neck. Her only accessory was a pair of spectacles that enhanced the impression of a serious, studious young woman. But underneath them were eyes shining with warmth, and a pretty, rounded face. Betty's physical appearance wasn't striking or showy. Nor did she have a big, outgoing personality to attract other people's attention. But her joy in Christ and her gentle, loving spirit did.

One former professor described her as "a presence so radiant of sincerity and inward beauty that its memory can never be effaced. Perhaps what most alumnae will remember … will be the serenity and faith with which she lived among us; a serenity born of the deep peace of her own soul, and a faith that was founded upon a Rock."[4]

---

3. *Missionary Martyrs*, p.44.
4. *The Triumph*, p.38.

To Die is Gain

Betty's faith was indeed founded upon a rock. In fact, the "rock" was the metaphor she chose to use in an autobiographical poem she sent to her parents during her second year at Moody. Despite her outward serenity, the poem shows that inwardly a fierce spiritual battle had been underway. It shows that like many young people who have grown up in Christian families, Betty too had faced times of doubt and uncertainty as she stood on the brink of adulthood. In the accompanying letter she explained: "This poem expresses the distress of soul and fear of mind that were mine before I surrendered my all – even inmost motives, as far as I know – to God's control."

Stand Still and See

I'm standing, Lord;
There is a mist that blinds my sight.
Steep, jagged rocks, front, left and right,
Lower, dim, gigantic, in the night.
Where is the way?

I'm standing, Lord:
The black rock hems me in behind,
Above my head a moaning wind
Chills and oppresses heart and mind,
I am afraid!

I'm standing, Lord;
The rock is hard beneath my feet;
I nearly slipped, Lord, on the sleet.

So weary, Lord! and where a seat?
Still must I stand?

He answered me, and on His face
A look ineffable of grace,
Of perfect, understanding love,
Which all my murmuring did remove.

I'm standing, Lord:
Since Thou hast spoken, Lord I see
Thou hast beset — these rocks are Thee!
And since Thy love encloses me,
I stand and sing.[5]

---

5. Ibid, p. 44.

Testing the Waters

As Isaac Page closed the meeting with a final prayer, John Stam found his eyes flicking again towards the young woman seated opposite him in the Pages' cosy sitting room. Her dark head bowed, she stayed in the posture of prayer for several moments beyond that last "Amen"; her eyes tightly closed, her knitted brow seeming to emphasise the sincerity of her prayers.

Betty Scott. A year ahead of him at the Institute, she was a firm fixture at the Pages' weekly meetings for the China Inland Mission. Everyone knew of her parents' missionary work in China, and her own intention to follow in their footsteps. In the brief conversations they had shared over tea at the end of the meetings, John had been impressed by the maturity of her faith and the strength of her calling to China, which by that stage was a settled conviction.

In fact, during her time at Moody, Betty had tried not to assume that God would call her to China. Although it was very much on her heart, she wondered at times whether the wrong motives were driving

To Die is Gain

her desire to return. Her parents were there, and it felt like home – but what if God wanted to send her somewhere else?

"Dear Father," she often prayed. "You know my heart. You know how much I love China, and its people, and long to be able to do your work there. But I truly want to be where you would have me. Please would you make your will clear to me, and guide my steps."

For a brief time, she wondered about Africa. Her heart was particularly moved when she heard about the plight of those suffering from leprosy, for whom so few seemed willing to care. It was a hard prospect indeed. "Such a ministry seems so Christ-like," Betty reflected. "Yet would I be willing to give up the dear prospect of China in order to serve God in that way?" After much wrestling in prayer, Betty resolved that she would. For how could she doubt that God knew what was best? If He should send her there, then that was His "good, pleasing and perfect will"... and she wanted nothing less. It was during this period of soul searching that she wrote these lines:

And shall I fear
That there is anything that men hold dear
Thou would'st deprive me of,
And nothing give in place?
That is not so –
For I can see Thy face
And hear Thee now:

*"My child, I died for thee.
And if the gift of love and life
You took from Me,
Shall I one precious thing withhold
One beautiful and bright
One pure and precious thing withhold?
My child, it cannot be."*

By the time John and Betty were getting to know one another, this time of uncertainty was over. Betty was surer than ever that God was leading her to apply to the China Inland Mission when she graduated from Moody. This being decided, she was determined to keep her feet firmly on the ground when it came to romance. Sure, she had noticed John; with his six foot two inch frame he was easy to spot as he strode around the college from one class to the next, or serving in the cafeteria. Although he was a year younger than her, he looked older than his age, and as she had got to know him better Betty realized that this maturity went deeper than his appearance. Like everyone else, she was struck by his godly Christian character and his obvious love for the Lord. Yes; she liked him. She liked him a lot.

Before Moody, before Keswick, Betty had certainly entertained her share of daydreams about love and marriage. She even wrote a poem, when she was eighteen, about the qualities she would look for in a potential spouse!

To Die is Gain

My Ideal

*I'll recognize my true love
When first his face I see;
For he will strong, and healthy,
And broad of shoulder be:
His movements will be agile,
Quick, and full of grace;
The eyes of Galahad will smile
Out of his friendly face.*

*His features won't be Grecian,
Nor yet will they be rough;
His fingers will be flexible,
Long, strong, and tough:
Oh, he'll be tall, and active
As an Indian,
With rounded muscles rippling out
Beneath his healthy tan.*

*His interest is boundless
In every fellow man;
He'll gladly be a champion
As often as he can:
Oh, he'll be democratic
And maybe shock the prude;
He will not fawn before the great,
Nor to the low be rude.*

*He'll be a splendid "mixer",
For he has sympathy;
Perhaps his most pronounced trait
Is versatility;*

*If Providence should drop him
In any foreign town,
He'd somehow speak the language
And find his way around.*

*He'll have a sense of humor
As kindly as it's keen;
He'll be a mighty tower
On which the weak may lean.
His patience and unselfishness
May readily be seen;
He's very fond of children,
And children worship him.*

*He will not be a rich man,
He has no earthly hoard;
His money, time, heart, mind and soul
Are given to the Lord.
He'll be a modern Daniel,
A Joshua, a Paul;
He will not hesitate to give
To God his earthly all.*

*He'll be, he'll be, my hero —
A strong-armed fighting man,
Defender of the Gospel,
And Christian gentleman.
Oh, if he asks a Question,
My answer "Yes" will be!
For I would trust and cherish
Him to eternity.*[1]

---

1. Both poems in this chapter from *The Triumph*, p.43 & 53.

To Die is Gain

Betty had grown up a lot since then; and besides, as she had told her parents, she would be content to be "an old maid missionary" if that was God's plan. But she couldn't help but smile to herself as she remembered the "ideal" of her girlish daydreams. How well the poem seemed to describe John Stam! She half dared to wonder. Could it be that God had brought John into her life for a reason? Might they have a future together ... somewhere down the line?

John and Betty both had good reasons for taking things slowly. Their future was uncertain, and both wanted to put God first and follow where He might lead them. Besides, their lives were so busy with studying, meetings and ministry, there was very little opportunity to spend time together, and never by themselves.

During his second year at the Moody Institute, John became even busier when he agreed to act as a temporary pastor for a small country church two hundred miles away from Chicago. He saw this as a good test to see whether he "could ever do anything for the Lord in China." For the remainder of his time at college, John faithfully travelled out to Elida in Ohio twice each month, to preach and encourage the congregation there. It was a great sacrifice of time and energy, but the spiritual hunger and the warm welcome John met with more than made up for that.

"We shall always remember his first appearance in our pulpit, and how pleased we were with his earnest message," wrote one grateful church member from Elida. "His kind, courteous manner, his zeal and fresh enthusiasm and his helpful sermons won us completely."

John was paid very little for this work; in fact, the salary barely covered his travelling expenses. But he didn't mind that; he wasn't doing it for the money. John took his responsibility to teach these people from God's Word very seriously, and prepared his sermons with great care. He also encouraged the congregation to memorise Scripture, as he tried to do himself. Sometimes he might give fifteen minutes at the start of a service to the sharing of special verses, encouraging others to contribute and suggest verses to learn together. He wanted them to see how relevant the Bible was to every area of their lives, and to store it up in their hearts.

Not only did John lead their services and preach, but he endeavoured to visit as many of the congregation as possible in their homes. This often meant long walks, but John was glad of the chance to enjoy the countryside after the noise and pollution of inner city Chicago. The people of Elida found him very good company, just as able to relax and share a joke as he was to teach them from the pulpit. Many of them came to see him as a close friend. He especially loved being with the families, and took every opportunity to teach the children Bible stories and songs.

To Die is Gain

On one weekend trip to Elida, John went out of his way to visit a family with three-month-old twins. He was captivated as he gazed down upon the two tiny, perfect bundles in their baskets, fast asleep. For some time he stood there, just looking, until the twins' grandmother wondered what he could be thinking.

"Such little tots!" he said, at last. "And you never can tell what lies before them in life."

After that he prayed for the precious babies, and committed them to the safekeeping of their Creator.

Other times, John brought along other students from Moody to help put on special services or to sing. John loved music and had a fine tenor voice. Sometimes he was able to recruit enough friends from Moody to form a quartette, and the Elida folk nicknamed them "The Happy Four." The name fitted: they were so full of the joy of the gospel, so eager to sing the glories of the Savior who died that they might be forgiven.

For sixteen months John served the church in Elida, and during that time he made a profound impression on that small farming community.

> *"Just to know him, to hear him sing God's praises, to be near him was such a privilege. His life was full of the promises of God, and we were so proud to have him for our friend!"*[2]

---

2. Quotations from *The Triumph*, p. 46-48.

Go Forward!

Betty graduated from the Moody Bible Institute in May of 1931, and immediately left Chicago for missionary candidate training in Philadelphia. If accepted, in a few months time she would be travelling to China with the China Inland Mission. The main concern in her mind was the medical assessment. The rheumatic fever of several years past had left her heart weakened, and sometimes she tired very easily. Would that render her unfit for missionary service overseas? She hoped and prayed not; but left it in the Lord's hands.

John missed her terribly. He longed to write to her, but felt something was holding him back. It didn't seem fair, when he had no idea whether they had a future together or not. Betty's call to China was clear, but he still had another year at college. He felt increasingly drawn to China himself, but he wanted to be sure, not just be led by his feelings for Betty. And even then, he would need to go through the missionary training himself, and get through the medical ... and then, after all that, they might want to send him to a completely

To Die is Gain

different part of China! Two years ago, Dixon Hoste, the director of the CIM, had sent out a particular appeal for young male missionaries who would be willing to travel and evangelize in the more dangerous inland regions of China. If John was asked to do that kind of work, it would be far better to stay single.

One afternoon while John was trying to concentrate on studying, with all these thoughts jostling around in his head, there came a knock at the door.

"Hello, John!" It was a man he knew only a little. "Sorry to interrupt you, but I don't suppose you might be able to type a letter for me?"

This wasn't an unusual request; John was a fast typist from his years working in business, and often helped friends out in this way. As he typed, the man began to open up to him about his own life. A former student at Moody himself, he had abandoned his own studies to get married. When John gently probed, it became clear that the man hadn't felt at peace about the decision, but had gone ahead anyway. Although he didn't talk openly about the details, there were tears in his eyes as he spoke about how difficult life had been since. John could not help but relate this sorry tale to his own situation.

Later he wrote in his journal about the struggle going on inside him.

"May 24, 1931. Betty is in Philadelphia now, but I have not been able to write her a letter. After much searching

of heart and of the Scriptures, I feel that the Lord would be displeased at my going forward in this direction ... I cannot move one step in her direction until I am sure that it is the Lord's directive will. I don't want to wreck her life and mine, too."[1]

Betty completed her missionary training that summer and, despite her fears, passed the medical, too. She would be sailing for China in the fall. The next edition of CIM's magazine, "China's Millions", featured a photo of Betty and a short testimony she had written.

"A missionary's daughter, brought up in China, I have always seen something of heathenism. But, although I knew the Lord as Savior so early that I cannot remember any definite decision, many experiences and battles followed before I truly accepted the Savior as my Lord.

During my school years, I prayed that if it were God's will, nothing might prevent me from returning to China as a missionary. My parents and others prayed thus about me, too. I, myself, first made this prayer in 1925 at Keswick, where I received this verse, 'For to me, to live is Christ and to die is gain.' Since then, other lines of activity, even other fields, have come up before me – and I cannot say they were not of the Lord – while even as recent as September of this year, it was uncertain whether, for physical reasons, I would be accepted at all.

But 'being in the way, the LORD led me' (Genesis 24:27). He, who made me willing to serve Him anywhere, has closed all other doors and opened this one – service under the

---

1. *Missionary Martyrs*, p. 63.

To Die is Gain

> *China Inland Mission in China. For this I praise his name; for I love China and believe it is the neediest country — just now, needier than ever.*
>
> *I will make mention of his faithfulness, which is great. Praising the Lord is, I believe, the only thing in the world worth doing. And praising Him involves bringing in other members of his body — those now in heathenism — to Him.*[2]

Betty would be sailing from the West Coast to China, so she and John were able to arrange to spend a day together in Chicago as she was travelling across the country. They spent much of it down by the lake, talking and praying together. The happy hours passed all too quickly. Both were honest about their feelings for one another, but determined to put God first. It was hard, knowing that they could be parting for a long time, maybe even years, without a definite commitment. John wanted to ask Betty to marry him, but he knew he wasn't free to do that ... not yet.

As it was a Monday, they went together to the CIM prayer meeting at Isaac Page's home in the evening. It was just like old times. Of course, there was much excitement at the prospect of Betty's imminent departure, and many wanted to talk with and pray for her. After the meeting, John asked if he and Betty could spend a few minutes with Isaac, in private.

Sitting beside Betty on the couch, John began, rather awkwardly, to tell Isaac of his feelings for her.

---

2. Ibid, p. 67.

"Over time," he explained, quietly, "Our friendship has grown into something deeper. I have become very fond of Betty, and I am happy to say … that she returns these feelings. We want to leave the matter in the Lord's hands … but we hope, and pray, that He may be bringing us together."

Betty was quiet, but the radiance of her eyes as she looked up at John said more than words ever could. Delighted, Isaac prayed with the couple before they left. Then he waved them off from his doorway, watching the two figures depart into the dusk. He turned back to his wife.

"Dear John," he said, with a little smile. "He thought we hadn't noticed anything!"

John wrote to his father to explain how he had left things with Betty.

"Betty knows that, in all fairness and love to her, I cannot ask her to enter into an engagement with years to wait. But we can have a real understanding, keeping the interests of the Lord's work always first."

He added:

"From the way I have written, you and Mother might think that I was talking about a cartload of lumber, instead of something that has dug down very deep into our hearts. Betty and I have prayed much about this, and I am sure that, if our sacrifice is unnecessary, the Lord will not let us miss out on any of His blessings. Our hearts are set to do His will. But this is true, isn't it, our wishes must not come first?

To Die is Gain

> *The progress of the Lord's work is the chief consideration. So there are times when we just have to stop and think hard."*[3]

Back home in Paterson, Peter Stam finished John's letter and looked up at his wife as he laid it down on the table.

"Those children are going to have God's choicest blessing!" he exclaimed, fervently. "When God is second, you will get second best; but when God is really first, you have His best."

As Betty sailed to China to begin her language study, John settled back into his final year at Moody, working harder than ever. On top of his studies and his pastoral responsibilities in Elida, he still picked up part-time work whenever he could to help pay his college bills. Although things were tight, God always seemed to provide what he needed … just in time.

"The Lord has wonderfully taken care of me all through my stay here at Moody's," John reflected, writing to his brother Harry in Africa.

> *"The classroom work is blessed, but I think I have learned even more outside of classes than in them."*[4]

Even in the lead up to his graduation, John had cause to praise God for another unexpected answer to prayer when he found himself completely out of money. There was no way he could afford a new suit for the ceremony,

---

3. *The Triumph*, p. 55.
4. *Missionary Martyrs*, p. 66.

but now it seemed that he wouldn't even be able to pay the tailor for repairs to his old one. John had already left the suit with the tailor, and felt very uncomfortable when he went to pick it up.

"I'm so sorry," he said, embarrassed. "I'm going to have to ask you to wait on that sixty cents I still owe you. I promise I'll pay you as soon as I can."

Later that day, John got round to opening a package he had picked up from the post office on his way to pick up his suit. It hadn't occurred to him at the time that there might be money in it! But sure enough, along with some other things, there was a dollar note. Enough to pay the tailor and get a needed haircut before graduation! Elated, John wrote in his journal that night:

> "I won't have a new suit for graduation, but I'll have the Lord's grace instead, and that's enough! Hallelujah!"[5]

The suit and haircut were even more important since John had a major role to play in the graduation ceremony for his class. He had been given the honor of addressing the graduates and the hundreds of other guests who would be gathered there that day. Characteristically, John had put a lot of time and thought into what he would say. He used it as an opportunity to appeal to his fellow believers to reach out with the gospel, both at home and abroad. He gave his address the title: "Go Forward!"

---

5. Ibid, p. 70.

To Die is Gain

John's classmates looked up at the tall figure on the platform in admiration as he spoke to them that day; he was "like a prince among men". Many of them never forgot the message he spoke on April 21st, 1932. Many of them never forgot the passion for souls that was evident not only in John's tone of voice and manner, but more than anything in the kind of life they had seen him live among them over the last three years.

John spoke of the difficulties of spreading the gospel in that present time, not only overseas but also at home in the U.S., where a once Christian society was becoming increasingly godless and moral standards were slipping away. Yet he challenged his audience to press on with their task.

"Shall we beat a retreat, and turn back from our high calling in Christ Jesus; or dare we advance at God's command, in face of the impossible?" he asked them, boldly. "Let us remind ourselves that the Great Commission was never qualified by clauses calling for advance only if funds were plentiful and no hardship or self-denial involved. On the contrary, we were told to expect tribulation and even persecution, but with it victory in Christ.

"Friends, the challenge of our task with all its attendant difficulties is enough to fill our hearts with dismay. And if we look only to ourselves and to our weaknesses, we are overcome with forebodings of defeat. But the answering challenge in our Master's command to go forward should fill us with joy and with the expectation of victory. He knows our weakness and our lack of supplies; He knows the roughness of the way, and His command carries with it the assurance of all we need for the work. The faithfulness of God is the only certain thing in the world today, and we need not fear the results of trusting Him.

"Our way is plain. We must not retrench in any work which we are convinced is in His will and for His glory. We dare not turn back because the way looks dark. Of this we may be sure, that if we have been redeemed by Christ's blood, and are called into His service, His work done in His way and for His glory will never lack His support."

John went on to remind his listeners of the millions of unreached Chinese souls that passed into eternity every month.

"We must bring them that message that will deliver them from the power of Satan and bring them into the glorious liberty of the children of God."

"People of God, does it not thrill our hearts today to realize that we do not answer such a challenge in our own strength? Think of it! God Himself is with us as our Captain; the Lord of Hosts is present in person in every field of conflict to encourage us and to fight for us. With such a Captain, who never lost a battle, or deserted a soldier in distress, or failed to get through the needed supplies, who would not accept the challenge, to 'Go forward, bearing precious seed!'"[6]

---

6. *The Triumph*, p. 57-59; *Missionary Martyrs*, p.73.

To China at Last

The two young men flopped down on the grass with relief, weary after their climb. But the view was worth it. From the top of Garret Mountain one could see not only the whole of Paterson, but even as far as Newark and New York. For several minutes the two friends sat in silence, drinking in the spectacular view and filling their lungs with the fresh mountain air.

Soon John would be leaving this place; firstly for his missionary training in Philadelphia, and then, God willing, for service with the China Inland Mission. Looking at John's fixed profile, his friend Tom wondered what he was thinking. Perhaps he was feeling nostalgic as he faced the prospect of leaving all this behind.

But some time later, when John spoke, it was clear that his thoughts had been far away from New Jersey.

"Just think, Tom," he said, with a shake of his head. "There are scores of cities in China, as large as this one, in which they don't have the gospel."

To Die is Gain

To his great relief and excitement, on July 1st, 1932 John was accepted for missionary service in China. A flurry of activity followed as John prepared for his departure; buying and packing needed supplies, seeing to physical necessities like dental work, eye tests and such like, besides taking on numerous speaking engagements. Many local churches and Christian groups wanted him to visit to give his testimony and talk about his call to China. John was glad of every opportunity he had to speak of Christ and share his concern for the unsaved people of China. Hopefully he could encourage many others to give to overseas missions, whether it be their money, their prayers or even themselves!

In the midst of all the busyness, John wrote to Betty. After much prayer and soul searching, he finally felt that he was free to ask her to marry him. God had opened the door for them both to serve God in the same country, with the same mission agency, and after many months of praying and asking for guidance, John could see no obstacle in their way. He sent off the letter with happy anticipation, hoping for a reply before he set sail in September.

However, no reply came. Not even a friendly line to put his mind at rest. By the time his departure from Paterson came around, John had begun to worry. Had he presumed too much? He was so sure of the strength of his own feelings for Betty, it had not occurred to him that hers might have changed. In his heart, he knew it was unlikely, but nonetheless the silence was unsettling.

On September 8th, a large group of family, friends and well wishers gathered at the train station in Paterson to wave John off. Before he left them, they had a short time of singing and prayer. Many from the Star of Hope mission were there to see off the young man who had served so faithfully there. It was an emotional parting, and if John had felt any less certain of his call to China it would have been very hard to go. But his heart and mind were firmly set upon the course that lay ahead of him.

"Goodbye!" he called, leaning out of the carriage window as the whistle sounded and the train began to pull away slowly from the platform. As his eyes singled out his own family amongst the crowd, he felt overwhelmed with thankfulness. Where would he be now without their faith and loving support? His eyes misted over, but his smile was broad. "Goodbye! I'll write soon! God bless you!"

Before John set sail for China, he travelled to Chicago to bid farewell to friends from college, and to the beloved church family he had pastored at Elida in Ohio. He then spoke at two conferences before crossing Canada by rail to Vancouver, from where he was due to sail on the 24th of the month. During his journey, he finally received a letter from Betty, but it didn't contain

To Die is Gain

the answer he had hoped for. On the contrary, it seemed that she had heard nothing from him for some time, and had certainly not received his proposal.

"I do hope my letter gets through to her," John wrote in his diary that night. "However, the will of the Lord be done. I have no good and no desire beyond Him. But I do believe that He will give me Betty on the way."[1]

Before he departed for China that September, John had received an invitation to spend his final weeks quite differently. A large group of Christian friends had invited him to join them on a cruise to Bermuda and other interesting places, but it hadn't felt right to John. He didn't want to judge anyone else's decision, but as he explained, "It might be misunderstood, in light of the privations many missionaries are suffering, if I went on a cruise as luxurious as that one is to be." So John's first experience on the sea was his journey aboard the Empress of Japan, sailing third class to China along with five other young men who were to serve with the CIM. The new missionaries were under the care of a returning missionary couple, Mr. and Mrs. Windsor.

The voyage would last more than a fortnight, calling at several other ports on its way to Shanghai. The missionaries soon realized that there was a mission field right there on the ship, amongst their fellow travellers. They set up daily meetings for Christians on board, where they would pray and sing together and

---

1. *Missionary Martyrs*, p. 77.

John & Betty Stam

share from God's Word. All were welcome, and many of their fellow passengers were glad of the opportunity for fellowship and encouragement. Others were more cynical and a few, including another group of young men, openly scoffed at their religious zeal. They were there to have fun and enjoy themselves, not to be preached at!

One day, John was busy typing a letter in the dining room when he was approached by an Indian man, a Sikh. John had noticed him around the ship, as he stood out with his distinctive turban and thick black beard. The man smiled and introduced himself to John, speaking in slow, careful English.

"I see that you know how to type. Would you be prepared to type a letter or two for me, please? Perhaps tomorrow?"

"Certainly," John replied, warmly. "I can do them for you this evening if you like."

The man thanked him, and turned to go, but John was keen to make more of this opportunity.

"You seem to be a religious man," he observed, politely.

"Oh yes," the man replied. "I am from India, but I am a Sikh. Many in my country practice idolatry, but I have been enlightened. Instead, I follow the One True God."

"I believe in the One True God of the Bible," John replied, boldly. "That is why I am here. I'm on my way to China as a missionary, to tell people there about Him and his Son, Jesus Christ. Have you heard of Jesus?"

To Die is Gain

The Sikh nodded, interested.

"Yes, I have heard of Jesus," he answered. "But I do not know much about him."

He listened intently while John explained, as simply as he could, who Jesus was and why He came, to take the punishment for our sin upon the cross.

"The Bible teaches much more about Jesus," John told him. "If I were to give you a copy, would you read it?"

"I promise that I will," the man replied. "And when I return home to India, I will send you a copy of our sacred book in exchange."

The following day, the travellers enjoyed a short break from their journey when the ship docked in Honolulu, Hawaii. There, John had promised to pay a visit to a friend from Moody, Ethel Chong, who lived in Honolulu with her family. But he was surprised and delighted to see her waving from the dock when they arrived, having come with a group of friends to meet him off the boat. They took John and his fellow missionaries on a whirlwind tour of their beautiful island, which was followed by a delicious Chinese feast served by Ethel and her family. Later that evening the Windsors spoke at a Christian meeting, and the new missionaries were also invited to share their testimonies.

A few days later, the ship docked again at Yokohama, Japan. While John and his companions enjoyed a day of sightseeing in Yokohama and Tokyo, some of the other young men onboard the ship spent the day going from bar to bar, drinking heavily. These were the same men who had openly mocked the missionaries for their faith. Yet when everyone re-boarded the boat, several of these men seemed fed up and depressed. Still suffering the effects of the alcohol, a group of them struck up a conversation with John and his friends when they met on the deck.

"I'm sick of it all," one of them admitted, miserably. "I didn't even enjoy today."

His friend nodded. "We had a pretty rotten time of it," he agreed. "I don't know why I do it, but I feel like I just can't stop myself sometimes." He looked at the young missionaries with an expression that was almost wistful. "You fellows aren't like that. You seem so free."

Such an opportunity to speak of the gospel was too good to miss. Gladly, John and the others began to share of the freedom that comes from having sins forgiven and the joy of knowing God personally. It was only a short conversation, for the men were still half drunk and John didn't know how much they really took in. But who knew what God might bring about in their lives in the future? The young missionaries were grateful for the opportunity they had to share something of their hope in Christ, and later John reflected on what those men had said. He thought particularly about the comment that the Christians "seemed so free." "And free we are!" he wrote in his diary. "Not free to go into sin – even they didn't enjoy that – but free from sin with the remorse it brings, and able really to enjoy ourselves."[2]

---

2. Ibid, p. 81.

To Die is Gain

John had received a letter during the stop off at Yokohama. It was not from Betty as he had first hoped, but from her father, Charles Scott. Betty's father had visited John during his missionary training in Philadelphia, and liked him very much. He knew that John wanted to marry his daughter and approved wholeheartedly. But in his letter, Charles gently forewarned John that Betty was feeling confused about their relationship. Having not heard from him in some time, she simply didn't know what to think. Poor Betty! John was eager to set her mind at rest, but until the ship arrived in Shanghai there was nothing he could do but commit the situation to God in prayer.

Betty had not had an easy few months. Upon her arrival in China, she had originally been assigned to the city of Fowyang, in Northern Anhwei. Beginning her outreach work there amongst the women, Betty was encouraged by how quickly she was able to pick up the Chinese language, with much of it coming back to her from her childhood. It was far easier for her than for those who had to learn it from scratch. But she had hardly begun to settle before a crisis meant that all the female missionaries were ordered to leave the district. After thirty-seven years of service in the Anhwei province, a senior missionary, the Rev Henry Ferguson, had been taken captive by Communist bandits. With concerns about the safety of the other missionaries, Betty and her companions were relocated to a temporary mission station in Wuhu. They had no idea when or if they would be able to go back.

In the midst of this discouragement, Betty was glad of the opportunity to meet up with her parents in Shanghai when they returned from furlough. However, after travelling to meet them there she was disappointed to find that their journey had been delayed, and the message they had sent to let her know had never reached her. Betty felt rather despondent as she returned to her temporary home in Wuhu. Her missionary efforts seemed to have ground to a halt, and she couldn't understand why she hadn't heard from John in so long. She felt lonely and confused. Everything seemed uncertain, but she knew that God was in control of her situation and that she needed to wait on Him.

As the *Empress of Japan* finally approached the coast of China, John's excitement was mounting. He stayed out on the deck, determined to take in every sight and sound and smell. Miles before the coastline could even be seen, he noticed that the sea became very dirty. The ship's steward explained to John that it was silt from the Yangtze River, pouring into the ocean from the river's mouth just beyond Shanghai. When the ship docked, it was past ten o'clock in the evening, so the decision was made not to disembark until the following morning. John had one more night to wait before he would set foot on Chinese soil at long last!

To Die is Gain

Early the following day he was back out on deck watching all the noise and bustle of the busy harbour. He noticed a little Chinese houseboat moored right beside the ship, and looking down from the deck he could see the family who lived there going about their morning business. The mother, cooking breakfast over a small fire on the bottom of the boat. A teenage son, packing up the bedding he had been sleeping on upon the deck, rolling up his blankets to be stowed away for another day. A little girl, lowering a rag into the dirty sea water and using it to clean her face and feet. Her mother did the same when she needed to clean a dish.

In spite of himself, John was shocked by their poverty, and that of the many beggars he could see around the jetty. People huddled together, dressed in little but rags. He was suddenly conscious of the good European clothes he was wearing.

"Why, I must look to them like a regular millionaire!" he thought, uncomfortably. "But how best to help people like this? I could hand out the few dollars in my pocket but how far would that go? There must be thousands of beggars in China!"

As he mulled it over, he reminded himself that what they needed most of all was the gospel of Jesus Christ. Money would only help them for a little while, and then they would be poor again. He prayed that God would help him to have concern for these people's material and spiritual needs. He prayed too that he would never

John & Betty Stam

become accustomed to their poverty and suffering but be filled with compassion for them, like Jesus.

Once the passengers were transported to the customs dock aboard a small steamer, the missionaries were taken straight to the Shanghai base of the China Inland Mission, and there John met with a wonderful surprise. When he asked after Betty, to his amazement he was told that she was right there in Shanghai. He could see her later that day!

Betty had been ill with tonsillitis and had to travel back to Shanghai for a third time that fall to be treated by a doctor there. She had no idea that John was due to arrive, having heard nothing from him in months; but by God's wonderful providence, there she was at just the right time.

The reunion might have looked unremarkable to an outsider, but when John and Betty came face to face later that day their hearts were fit to burst with relief and joy. Once they had the opportunity to speak alone, all Betty's doubts were put to rest. John explained about the lost letter containing his marriage proposal, and assured her of the constancy of his feelings. Now that he was there in person, he wasted no time in asking for her hand in marriage, and of course, Betty was delighted to accept!

> *October 12, 1932, Diary of John Stam*
> *Hallelujah! Wonders never will cease. Our Heavenly Father so arranged it that Betty was here in Shanghai instead of being away up in northern Anhwei. She had to have tonsil*

To Die is Gain

tissue removed and was told to come on down for that. And she has promised to be my wife. How I do praise the Lord for all His ordering and arranging. He will not fail those who wait for Him.[3]

---

3. Ibid, p. 86.

Blessings and Trials

John and Betty were able to enjoy six precious days together in Shanghai before they had to go their separate ways. Hearing of the engagement, all their fellow missionaries were kind and supportive, most importantly the field director, Mr. Gibb. According to the rules of the China Inland Mission, there had to be a waiting period of one year before new missionaries could marry, but Mr. Gibb assured John that after that time there was no reason at all why the wedding could not take place.

The happy pair went into the city to buy a wedding ring for Betty, a simple gold band. It seemed a sensible time to do it, as they had no idea when or where they would be married, nor whether there would be a convenient jeweller nearby at the time! John offered to buy his fiancée a diamond, but she wisely declined.

"I don't think it would give the right impression when there are so many poor here in China," she explained. "It might hinder my ministry to them."

To Die is Gain

Betty didn't need a diamond ring. She had John, and that was enough. But for now, the two of them would need to continue to be patient and put the Lord's work first, for when Betty left Shanghai that October it would be a full year before she and John saw one another again.

While Betty returned to begin missionary work in Fowyang, John was sent to Anking to begin a year of intensive language study. Both towns were in the Anhwei province, but they were 250 miles (four hundred kilometers) apart and divided by the great Yangtze River. The climate, the culture and even the landscapes were different, for while Anking was surrounded by lush green hills and wet rice fields, Fowyang was arid, the city bordered by flat brown plains and fields of dry wheat.

Betty was far more interested to find out about the spiritual harvest that was underway in this most unlikely of places. All the missionaries had been driven out of the area in 1927 due to the anti-foreign sentiment that was rife at that time, and those leaving had been deeply burdened by anxiety for the few believers left behind. What would become of them in the face of the Communist persecution they were suffering? Yet in spite of the opposition, God blessed that small church, and when the missionaries returned they were astonished to find that not only had it survived but it had grown! There were 250 regular attendees, with new converts being added all the time.

When Betty arrived in the fall of 1932, it was with another single missionary, Katie Dodd, and a couple with children, the Glittenbergs, who had been reassigned from elsewhere in China. They were to relieve Mr. and Mrs. Hamilton, long-time missionaries in the area who were due to go on furlough. Soon after their arrival, Betty, Katie and a native believer, Mrs. Liu, set out on an exploratory tour of the area.

"Anhwei is the flattest country you ever saw in your life!" Betty wrote to one of her brothers. "It's almost like the ocean when very calm, with only here and there a bunch of trees and houses which can't be seen far off, as the houses are mud and the trees dusty, like everything else. Sometimes the first we saw of a homestead was the bunch of brilliant red peppers, hanging up to dry against a wall. These and the persimmon trees, which have a glorious way of turning color so that every leaf is a different hue, ranging from all oranges and reds to green, were almost the only bits of live color that we saw all day. Everywhere the people were harvesting sweet potatoes, out of what looked like piles of dry dust. Whenever a little donkey trotted by, it raised a cloud of dust that could be seen for miles."[1]

The three women travelled in rickshaws, which was quite an experience. These were little passenger vehicles, each pulled along by a single man on foot. Since the rubber tires had worn very thin, every bump in the road could be painfully felt! Progress was slow, as it was tiring to pull a rickshaw in the intense heat,

---

1. *The Triumph*, p. 66.

To Die is Gain

and every so often the rickshaw men stopped to pick burrs off the tires.

The party stopped to eat in a small market town, heading for a local inn where they were shown to a small room within. Even indoors there was little relief from the flies. By now the unusual sight of the two white women had attracted quite a lot of attention, and locals crowded in after them to stare! The landlady tried to shoo them away. "Out! Out, come on, all of you. Give these ladies some privacy!" Still, a number of them managed to sneak into the back of the room before the door was closed, and stood grinning at the women as they ate, their eyes gleaming in the dim light. For once the door was closed they were left to eat their meal with chopsticks in near darkness, unable to see whether they were eating any of the flies with their food! Maybe it was better that way, Betty reflected wryly.

They spent the night in another village nearby, where there was a small CIM chapel. Local Christians were kind enough to bring them hot water and boiled peanuts for refreshment, but it wasn't the most comfortable of nights. Betty and Katie arranged their bedding in the loft above the chapel, but the sound of rats scurrying about was too much for Katie, who dragged her bedding down the ladder to sleep on one of the chapel benches below. "I heard the rats," Betty wrote afterwards, "but was too sleepy to haul my bedding down a rickety ladder, and resolved not to move since nothing had scampered over me yet!"[2]

---

2. *Missionary Martyrs*, p. 100.

John & Betty Stam

The encouragements of the following day more than made up for the trials of the journey. The weary travellers arrived in Yingshan, a large city where no foreign missionary had ever settled before, although the CIM had an outstation there. The hope was that Betty and Katie might soon be able to move there and have a ministry to the city's thousands of women and children. They made their way to the CIM premises where a native evangelist, Mr. Yang, lived with his family, and that afternoon were welcomed in the chapel by endless streams of curious townsfolk. Mrs. Liu, the Bible teacher who had accompanied Betty and Katie, was kept talking constantly, while Betty tried to chip in a few words here and there as she was able, handing out tract after tract. It was a promising start, and Betty couldn't wait to come back and start Bible classes for the women and children. A great many of them would need to be taught to read as well, so that they could study the Bible for themselves.

However, the missionaries in Fowyang soon faced trials and dangers as well as encouragements. Just a few days after Betty and her small party returned from Yingshan, the baby daughter of the Glittenbergs became very ill with dysentery, a severe intestinal infection. Mrs. Glittenberg travelled with baby Lois on the day long journey to the nearest hospital, but on the way their bus was stopped by rebel soldiers who commanded everybody to get off.

The soldiers then began going through each passenger's luggage, taking whatever they could find.

To Die is Gain

Clinging tightly to her daughter, Mrs. Glittenberg pleaded with the men who were rifling through her handbag.

"Please don't take that," she begged them. "All I need is the medicine for my baby. She's very sick, and without it she might die. I'm taking her to the hospital in Hwaiyun right now."

Her heartfelt plea had no effect on the callous soldiers. Finding the bottle of medicine, they opened it and sniffed it; realizing it contained alcohol, three of them drank the contents there and then. Afterwards, they boarded the bus and drove away, leaving the stranded passengers to fend for themselves. Thankfully, Mrs. Glittenberg had some money sewn into the hem of her dress, and with this was able to hire a rickshaw to transport her and Lois to the hospital. But it was too late for the baby. Whether she could have survived without that delay, the Glittenbergs would never know.

The death of baby Lois was deeply distressing for all the missionaries in the group, as well as her family. Betty admired the strength of the Glittenbergs' faith as they continued in the work to which God had called them. In a letter shortly after, she reflected: "Here in this work, you just have to trust everything to God, including your children, and know that He will do exactly what is best, and according to His will."[3]

A few weeks later, Betty stayed home from church to help Mrs. Glittenberg take care of her young son

---

3. Ibid, p. 106.

John & Betty Stam

Milton, who had also become ill since the death of his sister. At around two in the afternoon, two government soldiers abruptly entered the CIM compound and sat down in the courtyard. Later, the missionaries found out that these men were scouts, who had been sent ahead to find a suitable place for a larger group of soldiers to set up camp. Being the only man in the house at the time, the cook went out to speak to them, but one of the soldiers became angry and hit him. As the man ran off to get help, Betty bravely ventured out to speak to the soldiers herself.

"I'm sorry, but we won't be able to help you," she explained, calmly. "All our buildings here are in use. We have a girl's school here, as well as our missionary residence, and the other rooms are for staff who live and work here."

Her words had little effect, and neither did those of the gatekeeper or the teacher of the girls' school, Mr. Wang, when they returned with the cook. Soon the other missionaries and the schoolgirls returned from church and went inside the building that contained their classroom and dormitory. Only minutes later, two companies of soldiers, numbering some sixty men, filed into the compound and entered the downstairs of the same building. They quickly moved all the desks and tables out into the courtyard. Mr. Glittenberg was away in Shanghai, collecting his older children from boarding school, but a local native evangelist, Mr. Ho, tried to intervene on the

To Die is Gain

missionaries' behalf. Getting nowhere, he went to appeal to the city magistrate.

The magistrate was supportive when he heard that the soldiers had entered a girls' boarding school. "It is certainly not proper for the men to remain there," he agreed. "I shall see to it that they are off the premises as soon as possible."

The others were greatly encouraged to hear this on Mr. Ho's return, but they continued to pray fervently while the soldiers remained. The authority figures could be fickle, changing their minds easily, particularly if they met with resistance. Alarmingly, as they waited, the soldiers also began to poke around the school's kitchen, and even to peer into some of the bedrooms upstairs.

Suddenly, there came a sharp whistle and the sound of loud commands being given. Betty and her companions looked out of the windows to see two lines of soldiers standing to attention, and soon afterwards they marched out of the compound. The relieved missionaries spent the rest of the day "in a sort of joyful daze," as Betty put it later, praising God for His protection.

Hearing of these events back in the safer environment of his language school, John couldn't help but feel deeply concerned for his fiancée. But the cheerful tone of Betty's letters encouraged him. He wrote to his parents about the incident at the compound, asking for their continued prayers.

"I was especially glad to see the calm way in which Betty was taking all of these happenings. I do praise God for her. But the above will help you pray more intelligently for her and for us both when we get out into the work. One never knows what we may get into, but of course, we do know the Lord Jehovah reigns. Above all, don't let anything worry you about us. If we should go on before, it is only the quicker to enjoy the bliss of the Savior's presence, the sooner to be released from the fight against sin and Satan. Meanwhile, we can continue to praise Him from whom all blessings flow."[4]

---

4. Ibid, p.108 & 110.

Learning the Language

John may have faced less obvious dangers as he studied in Anking, but there were still concerns about the safety of the CIM missionaries there. There was plenty of anti-foreign sentiment within the city, and for that reason it had been decided that students at the language school should not walk around in public there. When John had the chance to escape for a walk, he had to exit the city from the north gate just a couple of minutes away from the compound, and walk in the countryside. Eager to learn all he could about the Chinese culture, he watched the local women as they washed their laundry in streams and ponds. Most of the women still practised the ancient tradition of foot binding, which involved tightly wrapping the feet from early childhood in order to make them smaller, as was considered desirable at the time. "It's pitiful," John wrote to his family back home, "to see these poor women, some of them under heavy loads, trying to hobble along on their bound feet that are little more than stumps."

To Die is Gain

He also watched the children out in the fields, not playing but hard at work, even the very smallest. They would rake grass into piles and tie it together into bundles, which would be attached to carrying poles and taken home to be burned as fuel. Despite their heavy loads, John was struck by the boys' cheerfulness. He nearly always got a smile from them, or a friendly salute.

The hills outside the city walls were covered with graves, everywhere John walked, piled one on top of another. He was shocked that these didn't appear to be treated with any respect, and there were even piles of coffins here and there, awaiting burial. It sobered John to think of all these people who had probably died without ever hearing about Jesus, the "Resurrection and the Life." It made him feel all the more eager to get out there and witness to the Chinese about his glorious Savior.

But there was a lot of hard work to do first. From Monday to Friday, John and his fellow students followed an intense program of language study, broken up only by meals, prayers and an hour outside to exercise in the late afternoon. It was exhausting, even though John was very accustomed to hard work. He found himself greatly in need of the slower pace of weekends, as he often commented in his journal. "Praise God for another weekend with its chance to draw a breath!" He continued to feel greatly aware of his own need to spend time alone with God, and fought hard to make it happen, as his journal testifies.

Oct 28. Oh that I may stay close to the Lord. It is so easy to live on the past or just in hope of the future.

Nov 2. Am succeeding in having some blessed times with the Word, the Lord enabling me to spend 1½ hours or more each day in my devotions.

Nov 4. May the Lord keep me, with all this busyness, very close to Him.

Nov 12. Gave my testimony tonight. It's rather late and I've not yet had all my time with the Lord. It's getting to be a bit of a fight to keep time out for Him. Oh, to know Him better.[1]

By mid January, the weather had become very cold. John often awoke in the morning to find that the water in his washbasin had frozen overnight! The students spent as much time as they could in the kitchen, huddled around the wood burning stove. But John refused to feel sorry for himself, and was determined that no one else should either. He told his family about the wintry conditions but was quick to reassure them of his wellbeing.

But if you hear anybody saying, "Poor John", just you stop it right away. We've just been full of praise to God here for good health and good spirits. And with all the discomforts of cold rooms, etc., I'd far rather be here in the Lord's will than at home in nice warm houses with hot and cold water,

---

1. *Missionary Martyrs*, p. 96.

To Die is Gain

> *etc. I've just been amazed how well I have been keeping, I've hardly even had a cold.*[2]

John was reminded of God's provision every night when he pulled on the warm woollen socks, the very same pair he had bought after finding a five dollar bill on the street in his moment of need, back in Chicago. How long ago it seemed, and how far away!

That month John celebrated his twenty-fifth birthday. On the evening of that day, January 17th, 1933, he wrote reflectively in his journal.

> *Today one quarter of a century of my life comes to an end. Tonight I have been much mindful of many opportunities missed. But I do thank God for those countless blessings all along the way, and look for his leading in the future. I give myself to Thee, Lord Jesus. Use me as Thy tool for Thy glory. Amen.*[3]

John was a deeply thoughtful and spiritual young man, but that didn't mean he was always serious. Neither were his fellow students at the language school, who loved a bit of light relief from their intense workload. That day, at the end of a game of basketball, John looked up to see the rest of the players suddenly sprinting towards him en masse. An intimidating sight! They all piled on top of the birthday boy, throwing him down onto the ground and rolling him over and over in the snow until everyone was soaked through, but too worn out laughing to care.

---

2. Ibid, p. 111.
3. Ibid, p. 115.

John & Betty Stam

Once they had dried off and were warming up around the stove, John was surprised and touched to be presented with several gifts. He knew no one had money to spare, and certainly didn't want them to spend it on him, but he still found there was a lump in his throat as he began to unwrap the first present.

"You shouldn't have," he said, tearing off the brown paper. It was a book. Hang on a minute, thought John. On closer inspection, it was his book. Not just another copy of one he already owned, but the very same copy, with the same creases on the cover! There was a stifled laugh from one of the lads as John looked up quizzically. Beginning to get the joke, John reached for the next gift with a wry smile. They were all his own possessions, smuggled from his room earlier in the day! By this time everyone was laughing, even John. "Boys, you really shouldn't have!"

In March of that year, John sat three language exams, as well as an oral test. The following weekend, he faced what felt like an even greater challenge, as for the first time he was to preach at the school's morning prayers ... in Chinese. He was very nervous about it the whole week, but once he had got through it successfully he felt ecstatic. He wrote his weekly letter home that afternoon:

Hallelujah! Phew, that's been safely accomplished. When we first began to study, and read what Hudson Taylor[4] said

---

4. See page 161 for information on Hudson Taylor.

> *about men preaching in Chinese six months after beginning to study, we smiled. But here it is just one day more than five months after I began to study, and I've already taken morning prayers. Praise the Lord.*[5]

At the end of the month, the Director of the China Inland Mission paid a visit to Anking, to meet each of the missionaries and decide where they should be sent. At the time, the Mission had work going on in fifteen provinces in China, each with different needs and challenges. Much thought and prayer went into deciding who should be assigned to where. Mr. Dixon Hoste arrived at the compound on a Monday and began his interviews on the same day. However, by the Tuesday, when John was due to meet him, Mr. Hoste was unwell with a heavy cold and was conducting the interviews from his bed. A hugely respected missionary, Dixon Hoste had been with the China Inland Mission for nearly fifty years, since first coming out to China himself as a young man, one of the well known "Cambridge Seven". He was now seventy years old, and when John entered his bedroom he was struck by how weary the director looked.

Hoste was a former military officer, who always maintained a perfectly upright posture, but that day John observed that "there wasn't a suggestion of the army about him, and he seemed much more like a tired old patriarch, who has wanted for long to lay his burdens down. As he sat there, the first thing that

---

5. *The Triumph*, p.73. For more about Hudson Taylor and the Cambridge Seven, see page 162.

came into my mind was the picture we get in Genesis of the Patriarch Jacob leaning upon the top of his staff and blessing his sons."[6]

He and John had only been chatting for a few minutes before Mr. Hoste broke into prayer, as though it were completely natural to him to bring God into their conversation. He asked for God's blessing upon John and Betty, before going on to pray for the wider work of the mission, for other missions, and for the native church in China, for a good fifteen or twenty minutes. John felt as though once the director began to pray, he had almost forgotten John had come to be designated! Once he eventually closed in prayer, Mr. Hoste spent some time giving John advice, man to man, on a range of subjects. John eagerly absorbed the wisdom of this great missionary statesman, which was delivered in a humble and gentle manner, without being the least bit patronising.

At the end of the hour they spent together, Mr. Hoste told John that he was going to send him to Suancheng, in the south of the province. There he would keep studying the Chinese language while beginning missionary work, helping an American couple, Mr. and Mrs. Birch. The hope was that after a short period in Suancheng, John would then be involved in setting up a new mission station in a city called Tsingteh.

Soon after the new missionaries had received their designations from Mr. Hoste, the time came for them

---

6. Ibid, p. 74.

To Die is Gain

to make their farewells and leave the language school. It was bittersweet to part, for strong friendships had been forged during those months, but each man was filled with excitement for what lay ahead, feeling that now their real work could finally begin.

New Horizons

John sailed to Suancheng on May 12th, after a month in Wuhu, along a small river that connected the two towns. A man stood waiting for him at the launch.

"You must be John," he said, warmly. "I'm George Birch. It's great to have you with us."

John shook his hand firmly, with a bright smile. Impressed by the warm, easy manner of the tall young man before him, George felt immediately that they would be good friends. As they walked towards the large CIM compound that would be John's new home, George told him more about the work in Suancheng. The mission had been in operation for some time and the ministry there was well established. One of the main areas of need was in their large children's ministry, and it would be John's task to oversee this work alongside a young Chinese Christian, Mr. Ho. There were children's classes held three times a week, and a lively service on Sunday evenings to which over a hundred young people came.

To Die is Gain

John was somewhat daunted by the prospect of engaging with these youngsters in a language which still felt very new. He wrote in a letter home:

> *It would be hard enough to hold the attention of such a rowdy lot of youngsters at home with a knowledge of my own language. But if I am to have anything to do with these little folk, it's not going to be any easier. So do pray for that.*[1]

John had only been in Suancheng for a few days before he and George set out on a ten-day tour of local towns and villages, armed with gospel tracts to share with people and praying for opportunities to speak to them of Christ. They left on foot, walking twenty miles on that first day along a dirt road that the rain soon turned into a wet swamp. The mud turned out to be something that John had to get used to! Later they swapped their heavy shoes for straw sandals, which soon got soaked through but at least didn't get weighed down with caked-on mud. It was always a relief to reach an inn where they could get cleaned up and enjoy a night's rest. But despite the challenging conditions and physical exertion, gospel opportunities made the trip more than worthwhile. Everywhere they stopped, the two men found people interested in hearing from them. They knew it was mostly just because they were foreigners, but what did that matter? People gladly accepted gospels and tracts, and listened as George preached to them. John wrote to his supporters that

---

1. *Missionary Martyrs*, p. 126.

several thousands of people must have heard the gospel during that trip, many of whom said they had not heard it before.

"This is the type of work I hope to be doing for the years to come," John wrote, happily. "Getting out into the country, helping to build up the few struggling saints here and there, and preaching to the heathen in the towns and villages about, and in every tea shop along the road."[2]

A few weeks later, at the end of June, George Birch and his wife Grace left Suancheng to spend two months in the mountains. It was a common practice for Chinese missionaries, who worked tirelessly throughout the year, to retreat to the cooler mountain regions or to the coast for a few weeks during the hottest part of the summer. John could have left too, especially as he had received an invitation from Betty's parents to join them at their seaside retreat. But since he had been in Suancheng such a short time, he declined, preferring to stay and continue being immersed in the language. It left him in a position of some responsibility, for he would be the only missionary remaining on the compound!

Those nine weeks certainly did immerse John in the Chinese language, as he continued to carry out the children's work, join in with the church services and converse each day with the natives who lived on the compound. He was also bold enough to get out

---

2. Ibid, p. 134.

To Die is Gain

and about with gospel tracts in hand, taking whatever chances he had to speak to people about Jesus. Often he felt frustrated by his limited vocabulary, particularly when he spoke with the young people who would often seek him out – if only to stare at "the foreigner". Not only was his vocabulary limited, but he still only understood a fraction of what they said; they seemed to speak so fast! Nevertheless, he was glad to be able to say what little he could, and to give them more in written form. With the younger children, he was able to teach them gospel choruses and songs full of biblical truth.

Not only did John keep up all these areas of ministry, but, ever practical, he also tended the Birches' garden while they were away. Being new to the hot climate, John wasn't sure how to store the potatoes he harvested and sadly lost a good portion of the crop. However, he was able to can other fruits and vegetables, and even made several batches of jam!

Sometimes John did struggle with feelings of loneliness during those weeks, and he waited eagerly for letters from friends and family. Every time he ventured out on the streets he would hear the cry of "Foreigner!" in Chinese, which increased his sense of being different, an "alien". But as always John sought his comfort in his relationship with his Father God, and assured his supporters that the Lord was indeed giving him great peace and joy.

At the end of those nine weeks, he was asked to lead worship and to preach for the first time at the

John & Betty Stam

Sunday service of Suancheng's largest Chinese church. John was hesitant, feeling that his language wasn't up to it yet. But he always had a hard time refusing any opportunities to preach the gospel, so when Pastor Li insisted he soon agreed to do it. The whole week leading up to it, John battled with feelings of inadequacy. Several situations arose where his language proved to be insufficient, and the midweek children's meeting was the most challenging yet. Some of the children even began to mimic him. Thankfully, when the Sunday came around John felt very aware of the Lord's help, and was able to teach the Bible to the Chinese congregation in a way that was clear and faithful.

When the Birches returned, John was able to throw himself into language study more fully once again. He was determined to pass his second language exam before he left to get married in the middle of October. It wasn't always easy to focus in the intense heat; but although the local Chinese declared that this was one of their hottest summers for years, John was pleasantly surprised with how well he found he could cope. "I've been well able to sleep and to study, while even a lot of the Chinese during the hot weather say they can't do anything," he wrote home. "So praise the Lord indeed!"

John couldn't wait to see Betty again – and this time to make her his wife! The last few months had been particularly challenging for the missionaries in Fowyang. John had received news that a bandit army had laid siege to the city, trapping its inhabitants inside

To Die is Gain

the city walls. After several days of the siege, there began to be concerns about food shortages. A group of soldiers who were sent out to drive off the bandits ended up joining forces with them. It took the government in Nanking to intervene, sending airplanes to bomb the bandit forces so that they soon scattered and the siege was broken. John was immensely relieved and grateful to receive news of his fiancée's safety. He looked forward to the time, so near at hand, when they could face these dangers together. Even Betty's journey home to her parents in Tsinan, to prepare for her wedding, was fraught with peril. The presence of bandits in the area was still a concern, but Betty determinedly set out by riverboat, praying to God for protection. Along with all her possessions – bedding, clothes, books and a few other personal items – she took with her a young Chinese boy whom she had promised to accompany to school.

It rained solidly for the first two days of the journey. Unpleasant as this was for the travellers, Betty realized it was probably a blessing, for the Chinese strongly disliked being out in the rain and even the bandits were less likely to move around under such conditions. When she eventually reached the railway station at Pengpu at 11 p.m. to embark upon the next stage of the journey, there was an unexpected hold up. Although there was a train leaving at midnight, Betty was told that her bags must be checked by an inspector, who only worked day shifts. She and her young travel companion made their way to a Presbyterian mission station nearby where they were allowed to spend the night. The following day, she was treated with great suspicion when she returned to have her luggage inspected. Customs officials apparently suspected that her sealed boxes contained guns or explosives, and would not be satisfied until all the contents had been checked and found harmless. At last she was able to board the train and continue her journey to Tsinan, arriving fifteen hours later, tired but happy, at her parent's home.

John took his language exams, written and oral, on the last two days before he left to join Betty in Tsinan. He spent Thursday and Friday completing the exams before moving his possessions out of the Birches' home and into the neighboring house that he and Betty would live in when they returned as a newly married couple. John was so exhausted that he had to go to bed halfway through packing for his trip, finishing the job early the next morning. He then travelled by boat to Wuhu. John was greatly encouraged that he managed to have a good talk with the boat owner and several others about the gospel, feeling that he could both understand them and make himself understood. Filled with joy and gratitude, he later wrote to his family:

> *I think I shall have to take a couple of days off just to praise the Lord and to thank Him, which also I should like to do for the following reasons:*

To Die is Gain

1. That I'm saved and in the Lord's service.
2. For excellent health despite the hottest summer here in years and a change in climate, too.
3. Great advance in the language.
4. Maybe this ought to be #2. That, God willing, I shall soon be returning with "my wife". I like that phrase, too.[3]

---

3. Ibid, p. 148.

The New Mr. and Mrs. Stam

It was exactly one year to the day since their last meeting when John and Betty were joyfully reunited at the Scotts' home in Tsinan. They were very glad to have two days to spend alone together before the rest of the wedding party began to arrive. Although many of their loved ones were oceans away, there were still good friends they had made in China who were there to share the couple's joy. Betty's close friend and roommate from Wilson college, Marguerite, was now a missionary nurse in Chefon, China, and was delighted to serve as maid of honor. Katie and Nancy, Betty's co-workers from Fowyang, were her bridesmaids, and John had as his best man his good friend Percy, a missionary and fellow student from the language school in Anking.

On Wednesday, October 25th, 1933, the day dawned bright and fair, without a cloud in the sky, nor any wind to stir up the dust. This was a blessing that enabled them to hold the marriage ceremony outside and so accommodate more guests. The tennis court on the mission compound had been converted into an

To Die is Gain

open air chapel for the occasion, with benches brought from the church and a red carpet lining the aisle. It was a beautiful setting, with trees lining three sides of the tennis court and from the fourth, a beautiful view over the distant hills. Friends had decorated the top end of the "chapel" with flowers, palms and ferns.

The guests arrived to arrangements of classical music playing on the gramophone. When the time came for Betty and her bridesmaids to walk down the aisle, a traditional wedding march was played on the piano that stood by an open window in the Scotts' living room, and could be heard clearly from there. The bridesmaids and maid of honor entered first, wearing lavender silk dresses and carrying bouquets of yellow chrysanthemums, followed by Betty on her father's arm. She wore a white silk dress with wide sleeves and a long, full skirt, the neck and veil trimmed with Brussels' lace. But what the guests noticed most was her radiant face as she smiled at her husband-to-be. At Chinese weddings, even among Christians, it was traditional for the bride to keep her head modestly bowed, but Betty looked right into John's eyes, not attempting to hide her happiness.

Writing to his parents later, John told them: "The wedding went off beautifully, or at least so everybody said. About the only thing I know was that Betty looked very very beautiful as she came down the aisle at her father's side. Then I led her to the minister and the words of that beautiful ceremony began." Although

John & Betty Stam

Peter and Amelia Stam were not able to be present in person, they were very much there in thought. John did not know then that back home in Paterson, his parents had risen at 2:30 in the morning to pray for the young couple at the exact time of the wedding ceremony.

When the service was over, everyone shared refreshments together at the other end of the tennis court; wedding cake and cookies, tea and fruit punch. Later, when the guests had left, the bridal party shared a time of devotions together, singing, reading the Bible and praying, before John and Betty left in the evening to spend the night at a nearby hotel. The following day they travelled by train to Betty's childhood home in Tsingtao. The Scotts still owned the house they had built in Tsingtao, and planned to retire there. But for two glorious weeks, it was John and Betty's honeymoon retreat. John wrote of their joy in his letters home.

October 27. This letter finds us at Tsingtao – a young married couple. Oh, the Lord has been so good in all the arrangements that we have just been praising Him all along the way. We're just having a most blessed time together. I've such a lot of things to tell you that I'm going to see if I can lay my hands on some typewriter around here before the Lord's blessings pile up so high that I shall forget a good many of them. Truly our God seems to go way out of His way to make His children happy.

October 31. Tsingtao is built on a big peninsula, or series of them, with many high mountains and lots of woods. The place in which we stay is on the side of a high hill overlooking the beach, the far peninsula, and the sea

> *beyond. It's just gorgeous, and Betty and I are daily enjoying our walks around the hills. The trees are just turning and the air has that delightful autumn tang to it.*
>
> *We've been out for meals a few times to some old friends of the Scotts here in Tsingtao. But most of the time we are out walking, at home reading, and just simply enjoying ourselves. Incidentally, I guess this is the first real vacation I've had with nothing to do for years and years.*[1]

A highlight of the fortnight was when a friend of Charles Scott lent the newly-weds his cottage in the heart of the mountains so that they could spend a night there alone together. It was in a stunning location, surrounded by the mountain peaks and trees displaying the first colors of autumn. In the morning John and Betty took a walk through a valley to visit a beautiful waterfall, surrounded by pools of pure, clear water. Having seen only two other people the whole walk, John and Betty took advantage of their privacy by laughing, singing and even yodelling at the top of their lungs!

Before they travelled back to Suancheng, John and Betty boarded a ship to Shanghai to spend a few days there. It was a far more luxurious journey than either were used to, for they were sailing first class – courtesy of Betty's parents, who had insisted on covering all honeymoon expenses as their wedding gift to the couple. Ever the missionary, during the voyage John recorded in his journal: "Beautiful day, sunshiny and calm. The only fly in the ointment was

---

1. Ibid, p. 153.

John & Betty Stam

that I didn't speak to anyone aboard the ship about his soul."

The days in Shanghai were busy ones, filled with a mixture of business and pleasure. There were necessities to be taken care of, such as seeing a dentist and shopping for needed supplies. The new Mr. and Mrs. Stam also had a wedding portrait taken by a professional photographer, attended several church services and prayer meetings, and spent time catching up with missionary acquaintances.

After a long and tiring journey back to Suancheng by sailing craft and then rowing boat, John and Betty were thrilled to arrive at their new home at last. Of course, everything was familiar to John, but brand new for Betty! They spent much of the first few days unpacking and settling into their new house, but certainly didn't waste time getting stuck into ministry. The evening after they arrived the mission's midweek Bible class was unusually well attended, which John wryly noted "was accounted for in part by the curiosity as to what the new bride looked like." Betty joined John in helping to lead the children's meetings which were held several times each week. It wasn't long before female students began dropping in to see Betty at home, and she was able to start a weekly Bible study for them.

John and Betty arranged to keep meeting up with a native language teacher to further improve their Chinese. Betty was very impressed by how far John had progressed with the language in such a short space of

To Die is Gain

time. She wrote to her in-laws: "I must say that John has gotten the language wonderfully in a year, both written and spoken. Everybody remarks on it. He has gotten idiom and tones especially well, and understands a great deal of what is being said." In the same letter she told them how they had visited a tailor to have fur-lined gowns made, in time for the colder weather. "You ought to see John in his Chinese garments! He looks taller than ever. And watch him gather his arms up under the skirts in the back, when he is going downstairs, for all the world like an old Chinese gentleman!"[2]

The couple ate their meals with Mr. and Mrs. Birch to save on housekeeping, but enjoyed many a quiet evening by their own stove, John at one end of the table with his books and Betty at the other. Having had a head start, Betty was busy preparing for her final language examination, which would complete the course of study that was required for missionaries with the CIM.

There were also opportunities for evangelism further afield. John took certain trips without Betty over the next few months, but at times she was able to accompany him. In December of 1933, they travelled to the outstation at Tsungchiup'u, where they held services in the chapel as well as two open air meetings, and walked around the town distributing tracts and visiting people in their homes. On the ten mile walk home, the missionaries took every opportunity to stop and share the gospel with groups of people they met,

---

2. Ibid, p. 158.

even holding an unplanned outdoor meeting in the village where they stopped to eat lunch. John wrote happily: "We finally arrived in Suancheng with every tract given out and every Gospel sold, and with a big blessing in our own souls."

At the time of the Chinese New Year, in February of 1934, John and Betty were able to make a longer journey to visit the place where they expected to relocate later that year, a region at the very south of the Anhwei province, around sixty miles south-west of Suancheng. It was an arduous trip which would involve covering some two hundred miles by foot and another thirty-five by boat, in the space of three-and-a-half weeks. The Stams were keen to see as much as they could of the area that had been in their thoughts and prayers for many months.

One of the towns they visited was Miaosheo, where they stayed with a widow named Mrs. Wang, who had been the first convert to Christianity in the entire region. She told them her story. Some years ago, a missionary couple, Mr. and Mrs. Gibb, had been passing through the area and were looking for somewhere to spend the night in Miaosheo. While Mrs. Gibb was still in her sedan chair, Mr. Gibb had begun to preach in the street. Mrs. Wang was among those listening, and sensing that this was a message of great importance, she had run home to fetch her husband to hear it too. It was the first time they had ever heard the gospel,

To Die is Gain

and they eagerly invited the Gibbs to stay at their house overnight. When asked later if she believed this new message, Mrs. Wang had replied: "I do not see how one could do anything but believe when told of such wonderful love." Mr. Wang had also put his faith in Christ.

When they left Miaosheo, John and Betty travelled on twelve miles across the mountains to Tsingteh, the city which was to be their base in a few months time. They spent a week there with a missionary couple, Mr. and Mrs. Warren, who would leave on furlough when John and Betty moved there permanently. Tsingteh had once been a wealthy city, a popular residence of noble families, but much of it had been left in ruins after the T'aiping Rebellion of the previous century. Although many parts of the city had never been rebuilt, there were still remnants of its former glory in evidence. To Betty, it felt noticeably wealthier than the other Chinese towns she had visited. She described the city and the mission residence in a letter to John's parents:

> *The people live in more comparative comfort, eat better food, and are probably more self-satisfied. Many live in old houses full of spacious halls, wonderful carved wooden beams and shutters. Even in the inns coming down we rarely encountered a single flea or pest – a thing unheard of in the north.*
>
> *The premises here are thoroughly Chinese, but big and roomy. We really have a fine street chapel at the front, and a comfortable place to live in the rear, made out of one of*

the old Chinese houses. It used to be an opium den, then a cloth shop in front and a private school behind.[3]

Unlike in Suancheng, the CIM's work in Tsingteh was not well established. The Warrens had been there only about a year, and before that missionaries had only stayed there occasionally. There were only one or two professing Christians in the town. Instead, its inhabitants tended to practise ancestor worship. John explained to his family back home how costly it could be for members of this community to become Christians.

For centuries back many of these people have been of the gentry class, with ancestors and relatives as officials at court to supply the means of living. Now they live on the proceeds of the clan property which is divided once a year. Anyone following the Christian doctrines and refusing to join in their ceremonies stands the chance of having his income cut off as well as being deprived the use of the family name. A farmer of the clan may find his fields taken away or his water supply cut off. So it is only the power of God that can work against such powers of coercion.[4]

When they left Tsingteh, John and Betty journeyed south, crossing the border into the Chekiang province to meet with believers in Chiki, and then travelling northwards for two days to visit the town of Changhwa. They spent a few days in the area, meeting different

---

3. Ibid, p. 163.
4. Ibid, p. 164.

To Die is Gain

groups of believers. One such meeting was with Pastor Cheng and his faithful congregation of eighteen members, and they were glad of the opportunity to hear his story.

Around thirty years earlier, Pastor Cheng's father, a schoolteacher, had bought a copy of the Gospels and the book of Acts from a bookseller who was passing through Changhwa. As he read them, he increasingly became convinced that they were true, and when the bookseller returned some time later, Mr. Cheng eagerly sought him out. "Is there more of this story?" he asked. "It seems as though they are only part of a larger book."

The bookseller was soon able to supply his customer with a complete Bible, to Mr. Cheng's delight. When the missionary Mr. Gibb visited the town, Mr. Cheng asked to be baptized. However, he had faced many hardships that had caused the other townsfolk to question the value of his Christian faith. Not long after he became a Christian, Mr. Cheng's eyesight began to deteriorate, and his neighbors were quick to pass their verdict. "This is happening because you won't worship our gods," they declared confidently.

The same was said when his grandmother died, and then when Mr. Cheng's son became seriously ill. Relatives longed to appeal to "the gods" on his behalf, but the boy would not allow it, for he shared his father's faith in Christ.

"No, we pray to the one true God," he replied firmly. "He will answer our prayers. Praying to idols will achieve nothing."

Wonderfully, the boy did recover, and went on to become the pastor of Changhwa. It was not an easy stand to make to live for Christ in that region; the Chengs had often been threatened with the confiscation of their land and property, but they remained faithful to the Lord. The testimony of such believers gladdened the hearts of the young missionaries.

The journey home to Suancheng, over the mountains, was a challenging one. Because of Betty's weakened heart, she couldn't walk endlessly and had needed to travel in a sedan chair for much of the trip. However, the only chair carriers they could find for that stretch of the journey were far from ideal; one quite an elderly man and short of breath, the other a young teenage boy. They had to cross a mountain pass, and while the ascent was straightforward, the two miles down again proved to be quite a nerve-wracking ordeal for John! "Believe me I prayed!" he wrote later. "Two carriers like that and such a descent. In places where the path doubled back on itself, the front man would be down one 'flight of stairs' and the back one up them, with Betty in the chair hanging over the 'abyss below'. I walked right close back of the rear man, and once threw my stick away and grabbed for the poles when he slipped a bit. I breathed a great sigh of relief when we were at the bottom."

To Die is Gain

Thankfully the final leg of their journey home was taken by boat, and the couple were able to relax for a day, reading and resting, before they arrived back in Suancheng late that night.

Becoming Parents

It was during that trip that Betty had realized with joy that she was expecting a baby. John was equally thrilled when she shared the happy news! However, when Betty's mother heard of the pregnancy she wrote back with grave concern about the effect such a rigorous journey might have had on Betty and her unborn child. With her typical optimism, Betty dismissed such concerns. On the contrary, she insisted, the journey had done her good! Still, the couple realized it would be wise to restrict the amount of travelling Betty did over the next few months, particularly given the problems with her heart.

John took another trip without her less than a fortnight later, to lead a mission in Kinghsien, twenty miles south-east of Suancheng. He and Pastor Ho, his co-worker in Suancheng, spoke at meetings morning and evening for a week in Kinghsien, before travelling on to visit three more CIM outstations where they were able to share the gospel in chapel services and open air services. The final outstation they visited was

125

To Die is Gain

in Nan Van, an area where bandits were currently very active. There had even been a recent kidnapping of two local children, who had been safely returned only after a ransom of nearly a thousand dollars had been paid. Because of this, there were often two or three armed men stationed at the back of each Christian meeting. John wrote:

> Really, some of the pictures these fellows presented were most incongruous, such as one fellow stomping up the aisle with a gun in one hand and a hymnbook in the other. And another, the schoolteacher, fur cap on head, several top teeth missing, a gun over one shoulder and a baby in the opposite arm.[1]

A few weeks after their return, John set out again for the southwest Anhwei province. He was eager to keep getting to know the area as well as he could before he and Betty moved there permanently. He stayed with friends they had already made, including Mrs. Wang in Miaosheo, where he was made very comfortable indeed. She kept her house immaculately clean and cooked delicious meals, all the while "hovering over" her guest, as John put it, "like the dear old grandmother she is."

There in Miaosheo, John worked alongside a native evangelist named Lo Ke-chou, who was set to move there with his family in order to help the Stams in their ministry in that region. The two of them visited many church members around the countryside, travelling between different villages to preach and distribute

---

1. Ibid, p. 169.

Christian tracts and gospels. They then travelled on to Tsingteh, deliberately going on the large annual market day when the streets were packed with people. "We sold many hundreds of Gospels and distributed thousands of tracts," John reported afterwards.

The highlight of that trip was the interest in the gospel that the missionaries found in a town called Peh Ti, south of Tsingteh. Another missionary, Sam Warren, who had never yet had the opportunity to minister in the area himself, had nonetheless asked friends in England and Australia to be praying for the town, asking that God would be preparing their hearts to receive the gospel. What John and Lo experienced there confirmed that these prayers had been wonderfully answered.

> *From the first it was evident that this town was a prepared place. I've never seen such friendliness and such courteous interest. The young students were first to gather around, and were quick to learn to sing our choruses. That brought more students, the schoolteacher, and the local official. All were very cordial and sympathetic. That night we had a most attentive audience in our inn which stood for an hour and a half and didn't seem to want to go home.[2]*

It was only when John and Mr. Lo finally announced that they needed to go to bed that the crowd reluctantly left!

They also met with opposition, however, in other places on their journey. In Kiang Ts'uen, a young

---

2. Ibid, p. 173.

To Die is Gain

man openly mocked John throughout his gospel talk, making the crowd laugh and completely undermining John's confidence. In another town, students from the government school made up a song called "Down with Jesus!" They tried to disrupt the meeting by tearing up tracts and pulling others away.

Still, John and Lo were not discouraged. At the end of the trip, John wrote to his supporters at home in the U.S.

We are looking forward with great expectations to our new field. It's a great open door, with its many villages scattered all through our parish of more than two hundred square miles, and we look to God to use us for his glory. Adversaries? —Yes, you know our great adversary. Besides him there is the same awful indifference you have to face at home. Added to that there's superstition among the ignorant and a type of nationalism among the educated young folk that scorns foreigners for everything except science and machines.[3]

When Betty was about seven months pregnant, in early July of 1934, the Stams moved temporarily to Wuhu. The CIM's local secretary, Mr. Walton, was in great need of a break, so he and his wife were going to the mountains for two months while John took over his responsibilities. With his experience in business, John was more than capable of doing the job, but administration was not something he particularly enjoyed. He would much rather be dealing with people than "juggling figures". But, nonetheless, he adapted

---

3. Ibid, p. 174-175.

John & Betty Stam

to the change of routine cheerfully, remembering it was for a good cause: "The dear old chap who holds this job down here for us all through the year certainly deserves our thanks. He's as truly a missionary as we are, keeping us supplied with money, food, etc, and he won't lose his reward."

As well as doing the secretarial work and bookkeeping, John kept up his language study alongside Betty. It was a swelteringly hot summer. Much of the Anhwei province suffered a drought, and temperatures soared, but John and Betty were thankful for some luxuries they hadn't had in Suancheng, such as electric fans, ice and ice cream, which helped a lot! Despite her advanced stage of pregnancy, Betty managed to cope with the heat well and even passed her fourth and final set of major language exams at the end of August. Just a few days later, at her doctor's suggestion, she was admitted to the hospital.

"I think it's a good idea if Betty gets a bit of proper rest before the baby arrives," the doctor explained to John. "It could be any time now. And we would like her to stay for a good three weeks after the delivery as well." He turned to Betty. "We do need to keep an eye on your heart, and it would be best to make sure it has properly recovered before you're up and about again."

John and Betty nodded their agreement. But despite the doctor's concerns, Betty could only feel excitement. Neither she nor John could wait to

To Die is Gain

welcome their baby into the world! Betty's sister Helen later wrote of the eager expectation with which they had both awaited the arrival of their child. She remembered vividly *"the anticipation and preparation for that little one. I realized during the months before she came that Betty was making more loving and caring preparation for her than I had over both of mine put together. She and John discussed many possible names for the baby, and their letters were crammed full of their love for her."*[4]

To their great joy, Helen Priscilla Stam arrived on Tuesday, September 11th, 1934, at 3:15 in the afternoon; a beautiful, healthy baby girl.

Clara Scott stood over the crib, gazing at her new granddaughter for some time before pronouncing her verdict:

"She looks just like you, John!"

John and Betty's eyes met and they laughed.

"You're not the first to say so, Mother!" Betty admitted, looking down at her sleeping child with unabashed pride. "I think she has his mouth."

The doctors had kept Betty and Helen in hospital for nearly a month before allowing them home, and now her mother had come to help for a fortnight. Betty was still weak, but she was enjoying her new role immensely.

"It is a real joy to take care of her," she wrote to John's parents. "We can't say she never cries. But during the night she sleeps soundly from 10 p.m.

---

4. *The Triumph*, p. 89.

John & Betty Stam

to 6 a.m., and most of the time from 6 a.m. to 10 p.m. too!"

Betty didn't pretend that their daughter was perfectly behaved though. She also described to her parents-in-law how much baby Helen protested when she was too wrapped up, wanting to keep her arms free. Like most newborns, she would also much rather be held than put down in her crib.

"Last night she howled and kicked so hard that she put her feet right through a little flannelette gown which Mother Scott had made for her!" she wrote. *"I'm afraid it was temper. For the minute anybody picks her up, she is as placid and serene as can be, with a slightly reproachful expression, as much as to say, "Why didn't you come sooner?" So we shall have to be very strict with her!"*[5]

John was equally besotted with his tiny daughter. Having been forewarned not to expect too much of a newborn baby in terms of good looks, he found her absolutely perfect.

"You should see our daughter!" he wrote proudly. "She really is the cutest little thing ... and would do for any baby show."

Although it was lovely to have some time at home together as a family, it wasn't long before John had to leave again for southern Anhwei. The plan was for the three of them to move to Tsingteh as soon as possible, and one of the main purposes of this trip was for John to find out whether it was safe to do so. This time his

---

5. *The Triumph*, p. 91.

To Die is Gain

companion was a fellow CIM missionary called Erwin Kohfield, who had been serving with his family in Tunki, about thirty miles south of Tsingteh, in what would be the closest missionary station to John and Betty once they moved. Unfortunately, the Kohfields had recently been forced to flee Tunki because of a Communist invasion, and now both John and Erwin had to seriously consider whether it was safe for their families to return to the area and continue their ministry to the people there.

In Tsingteh the two men met with the district magistrate, Mr. Peng. The area had been hit hard by drought over the summer months, and Mr. Peng admitted that they had been having some trouble with local bandits due to the shortage of food.

"Then perhaps we ought to leave it a few more weeks before we bring our families here," John reflected.

Mr. Peng nodded. "Yes, I would agree with you on that. However, we have many government troops stationed hereabouts, and I don't think the problem will persist."

"Of course, the other concern is that we would not want to risk encountering the Communists,"[6] John said, emphatically. Everyone knew that in the event of a civil disturbance, the foreigners would be the most vulnerable – and foreign missionaries the most vulnerable of all.

---

6. For information on Communism in China go to page 165.

On this point, Mr. Peng offered them the strongest reassurance. "Oh no, no, no! There is no danger of Communists coming here. As far as that is concerned, you could move here with your family right away, Mr. Stam. I can guarantee your safety, and in the unlikely possibility of any trouble at all, you can come to my yamen[7]."

The magistrate at Tunki was equally reassuring. "With the governor's troops in place, there will be no further trouble here," he pronounced confidently. "You and your family are quite safe to return. We can assure your protection."

John and Erwin were comforted by these assurances, but it was right to be cautious, particularly where their young families were concerned. Mr. Hanna, the CIM superintendent in Anhwei also travelled to the area to scout out the situation himself, and reached the same conclusion as the native officials. The Stams and the Kohfields were given permission by the CIM to move with their families to southern Anhwei. No one could guarantee their safety one hundred per cent; but then the same could be said of missionary activity anywhere in the world. It had not been a hasty decision, but one made after much prayer and careful consideration. John and Betty accepted this as the Lord's next step for them, and were confident that they could fully trust Him with their future.

---

7. A *yamen* is the headquarters or residence of a Chinese government official.

To Live is Christ ...
to Die is Gain

John and Betty packed up the small quantity of possessions they had with them in Wuhu, and travelled with baby Helen to Suancheng, where they spent several days helping with a short term Bible school and saying goodbye to the dear friends they had made there. They stayed with the Birches, and on their final Sunday service Helen Stam and the Birches' youngest son, John, were both dedicated to the Lord. The minister prayed that Helen Priscilla would grow up to be just like the Priscilla of the Bible, a help to the church and a blessing to other believers.

"It was very impressive, and very blessed," John wrote to his family of the service. "Both babies behaved wonderfully, our little Helen, when she was awake, quite enjoying herself doing nothing. She surely is a darling!"

Finally, with some sadness but also great excitement, the Stam family packed up the rest of their belongings and parted from their friends and colleagues in Suancheng. They travelled by bus to southern Anhwei, while their

To Die is Gain

household goods and possessions were transported the seventy miles to Tsingteh by wheelbarrow. The bus line ended some miles short of Tsingteh, so John and Betty were especially thankful to God for fine weather the following day as they travelled the rest of the journey on foot, over two mountain passes and through a wide valley into the town.

Once they had arrived, the weather soon turned very cold, and John and Betty were grateful for the two stoves that had been installed in the large, old Chinese house that was to be their new home. On their first Sunday in Tsingteh, on November 25th, they held a church service at which there were barely a handful in attendance; beside themselves and their household servants, one of the carriers they had hired and a visiting Christian from a neighboring mission, only a couple of locals wandered in and out again. The following Sunday, there were even less. John and Betty were reminded straight away that the work in Tsingteh was in its very early stages, but that made them feel even more convinced that this was the right place for them to be.

"We do praise the Lord for the privilege of being here," John wrote to Mr. Gibb from Tsingteh. "The district seems quite peaceful now, though there are rumors of rice-stealing in country places ... As to our work, we are praying that the Lord will help us to build wisely and truly here. We certainly do start from just about scratch."

John & Betty Stam

But John and Betty never had the chance to develop the work in Tsingteh as they had hoped. The end was coming. It was coming more quickly than anyone could have foreseen.

The Communist soldiers crossed the border into Southern Anwei just two weeks after John and Betty's arrival in Tsingteh. No one saw it coming. That morning of December 6th, 1934, the "Red Army" killed three city officials and fourteen of Tsingteh's headmen, each one the leader of ten families. They looted the town, taking everything of value they could lay their hands on. They arrested John, Betty and Helen Stam, along with more than twenty other prisoners.

Before the Communists left Tsingteh with their prisoners in tow, John was given one last chance to return home, under guard, to gather more food and supplies for the baby. The house had been thoroughly looted since their departure, and the servants were distraught. He took the opportunity to comfort the weeping women.

"Don't be afraid," he said to their maid Mei, gently. "God is on the throne. These little things do not matter – our Heavenly Father knows all about them. You go and sleep with old Mrs. Li tonight, and the cook will look after you."

At around four in the morning, the Communists began the twelve mile march to Miaosheo with their captives. Mercifully, they allowed Betty, weak from lack of sleep and food, to ride on horseback part of the

To Die is Gain

way, while John carried baby Helen on his back. There had been some discussion of whether to take the baby's life, the conversation being conducted right in front of her parents to further their distress.

"Why bother to kill her?" one soldier argued. "She's bound to die anyway – let's save ourselves the trouble." The decision held, and Helen's life was spared.

Before the Communists came, John had arranged to meet his friend Mr. Lo, the evangelist, in Miaosheo that very day. So Lo and his family, his wife and four-year-old son had travelled to the city the evening before and spent the night at Mrs. Wang's. The next morning at nine o'clock, an advance guard of soldiers was seen entering the city. When the news reached the Wang home, everyone was concerned.

"But are they government or communist troops?" Lo asked, anxiously. No one knew.

So Lo and Mrs. Wang's grown-up son, Wang Shi-Ho, made their way quietly to the main street in order to find out more. Immediately, they were spotted by a soldier, who pointed in their direction, shouting, "There's one! There's a headsman!"

Wang, who was indeed a headsman, quickly fled, but Lo was seized and questioned. The soldiers took him to the house of Chang Hsiu-sheng, a local doctor who belonged to the Miaosheo church. Chang defended him, explaining: "This man only arrived in town last night. Like me, he heals diseases … and distributes tracts in the country."

John & Betty Stam

Not seeming to connect this with Christian activity, the soldiers were satisfied and let Lo go. He bowed politely and walked away, his pace quickening as soon as he reached the back streets. He found the rest of his family and the Wangs waiting for him. Together they escaped into the mountains where they would spend the next two days and nights in hiding.

The rest of the Red Army and their prisoners arrived in Miaosheo later that day. The soldiers left the missionaries under the supervision of the local postmaster while they went off to plunder the town. The postmaster was frightened, but showed the prisoners some kindness, offering them fruit to eat which Betty gladly accepted. She had to try and keep up her strength to feed the baby. John used the time to write another letter to the CIM officials in Shanghai, having no way of knowing whether the first had reached them.

Miaosheo, Anhwei
December 7, 1934

China Inland Mission

Dear Brethren,
We are in the hands of the Communists here, being taken from Tsingteh when they passed through yesterday. I tried to persuade them to let my wife and baby go back to Tsingteh with a letter to you, but they won't let her, and so we both made the trip to Miaosheo today, my wife travelling part of the way on a horse.

They want $20,000 before they will free us, which we have told them we are sure will not be paid. Famine

To Die is Gain

> *relief money and our personal money and effects are all in their hands.*
>
> *God give you wisdom in what you do and give us grace and fortitude. He is able.*
>
> *Yours in Him,*
> *John C. Stam*[1]

John asked the postmaster to see that it was delivered.

"But where are they taking you?" the man asked, with grave concern. "Where are you going?"

"I don't know where they are going," John answered, calmly. "But we are going to heaven."

In the evening soldiers escorted them to the deserted home of a wealthy family, where the Stams were given a room to spend the night, with soldiers stationed outside. They left Betty unbound so that she could care for the baby, but John was tied to a bedpost in a standing position, unable to get any rest or comfort through that long, cold night. The family were left there until soldiers came to get John and Betty shortly before ten o'clock the next morning, ordering them to strip down to their long underwear. Betty was told to leave Helen behind, and could only pray that this might prove to be for their daughter's best. They now knew for certain the fate that awaited them.

They were taken, at gunpoint, to a place named Eagle Hill, which lay just outside the town. As they marched through the streets of Miaosheo, soldiers shouted out to the townspeople, ordering them to come and watch the

---

1. Ibid, p. 105.

execution of the "foreign devils". One of those watching in horror was Chang Hsiu-sheng, the doctor. While others hung back in fear, he was the only one who dared to speak out in defence of the Stams.

"They're good people!" he called out. "Please, do not do this wicked thing!"

Ignored by the indifferent soldiers, Chang bravely rushed ahead of them and fell on his knees.

"This must not be done!" he implored, raising clenched hands towards them, his heart pounding in his chest.

Furious, two soldiers grabbed him and dragged him to his feet.

"Are you also in league with these foreign devils?" they demanded. They took him prisoner, and later when his home was searched, the discovery of his Bible and hymnal confirmed their suspicions. For his courage, Chang too would later face the penalty of death.

John and Betty were executed that morning on Eagle Hill. John was ordered to kneel first. A soldier stepped forward with a large knife, striking him savagely. As his body slumped to the ground, Betty was seen to tremble before she too fell to her knees. Her suffering was short-lived, for the next moment she was struck with a sword, killing her instantly.

The two bodies were left where they fell, in a grove of pine trees on the hill. As the soldiers departed, the people of Miaosheo crept slowly back to their homes, overcome with shock and fear.

A Miraculous Rescue

Later that day, government troops marched into Miaosheo and opened fire on the Red Army soldiers. Both sides held their positions and few soldiers were killed, but at ten o'clock that night the Communists withdrew from Miaosheo, moving on about three miles to the next town. As they left, they set fire to the houses on their path.

That night a hush fell over the ravaged city. The people stayed behind closed doors, reeling from the horrifying events of that day. All alone in one abandoned house, a baby's hungry cries went unanswered.

Huddled together against the cold on the nearby mountainside, Evangelist Lo and the Wang family waited anxiously for news. Rumors had reached them that a foreigner had been taken captive by the Reds, but it was not until the next day that they heard the awful news: John and Betty were dead.

Over the low weeping of the women, Lo was the first to speak.

To Die is Gain

"We must go back and find their bodies," he said, his voice heavy with sorrow. "They must have a proper burial. The Reds are gone, for how long I don't know. But for now, let us do what we can for our dear brother and sister."

They made their way furtively back to the town, and Lo immediately began to ask where John and Betty lay. Many of the townsfolk would not talk for their fear of what the Communists might do; they no longer knew who they could trust. Finally he learned that the bodies lay on Eagle Hill, but as he set out in that direction, an old woman grabbed his elbow. She pulled him close to whisper loudly in his ear, "There's a foreign baby. A foreign baby left behind."

She pointed out the house to Lo and he ran there as fast as he could. Entering the house, he was met with silence, and wandered from room to room finding evidence of its recent occupation but alas, no sign of life. Lo was fighting back a mounting fear, when suddenly he heard a tiny cry which led him to a room off the courtyard. There she lay: little Helen Priscilla, hungry and bewildered but unharmed, snuggled safely in the warm sleeping bag her mother had tucked her into the previous morning. Pinned deep inside the layers of her clothing, Lo found two five dollar bills that Betty must have carefully hidden there, in the hope that anyone who found the child might use the money to help provide for her needs.

Taking the baby with him, Lo continued on to Eagle Hill to find the bodies of her parents there where the soldiers had left them. At first he could hardly bear to look at the mutilated corpses of his dear friends and fellow servants of Christ. Once he had seen the tragic spectacle with his own eyes, he returned to the town to get help. Leaving baby Helen with his wife, he bought two coffins on credit, and white sheets in which to wrap the bodies.

When Lo returned to Eagle Hill, it was with Mrs. Wang, her son, and a few others whom they had hired to help care for the bodies. Those who were there later testified that John's expression was one of unmistakable joy, and Betty's of complete serenity. By the time they had placed the bodies in the coffins and knelt to pray, a crowd had gathered around them. Once he had finished praying, Lo stood and turned to the silent group. Many of those listening wept as he spoke.

> *"You have seen these wounded bodies, and you pity these foreigners for their suffering and death. But you should know that they are children of God. Their spirits are unharmed and at this minute are in the presence of God. They came to China and to Miaosheo not for themselves but for you, to tell you about God and His love, that you might believe in the Lord Jesus Christ and be saved eternally. You have heard this message. Remember it is true. Their death proves that. Do not forget what they told you. Repent and believe the Gospel."*[1]

Lo's young son had become seriously ill from two nights of exposure out on the mountain, and was not fit to

---

1. Ibid, p. 112.

To Die is Gain

travel. Lo and his wife were torn about what was best to do, but given the threat of the Communists returning, they felt they must leave. As believers, and particularly after showing concern for the "foreign devils", they would certainly be in great danger. Lo was also anxious to get Helen into safe hands as soon as possible.

So they risked the journey, setting out on foot for Kinghsien in the north. They hired a coolie who carried their son and little Helen in rice baskets, on opposite ends of a long pole. The boy's condition became worse, and he did not eat or speak a word that whole day. The following day, Lo hired sedan chairs to carry them the rest of the way, and to their relief through the course of that second day their son began to improve, even sitting up and singing along to a hymn. Having been through the grief of losing two children already, his parents were overwhelmed with thankfulness that their son was spared.

At stops along the way, the Los managed to find native women who were able to breastfeed Helen. But when they arrived in Kinghsien, Mrs. Lo was able to buy powdered milk with some of the money Betty had left in the baby's clothing. This meant that she could feed Helen from a bottle on a regular three-hourly schedule. Given that bottle feeding was virtually unknown in China at that time, the fact that Mrs. Lo knew how to do it safely was another evidence of God's remarkable provision for Helen. Her son had been born in the Methodist hospital in Wuhu, and she still had the bottle he had used.

John & Betty Stam

It was Friday, December 14th, a week after the brutal execution of John and Betty Stam, that a knock came at the door of the Birches' home in Suancheng. George Birch opened it to find a woman there dressed in muddy clothes, exhaustion written into the lines of her face. It took him several moments to recognise her as Mrs. Lo. She clutched a child in her arms, bundled in a shawl, and as he stood there she held the bundle out to him, her eyes filling with tears.

"This is all we have left," she said helplessly.

Bewildered, George loosened the shawl around the child and found himself looking down at the sweet, sleeping face of Helen Stam.

Triumph

No one at the China Inland Mission had heard of John and Betty's capture until it was far too late. The first unconfirmed reports of a Communist attack reached officials in Shanghai on Monday, December 10th, four days after their capture. Once it was confirmed that John and Betty had been taken hostage by the Red Army, CIM representatives immediately began discussions with the Chinese authorities to find out all they could and determine what could be done to secure the family's release. The news of their capture was circulated around various parts of the world by telegram, and believers in many different countries were praying for their safety and release.

A letter telling of John and Betty's death finally came to Mr. W. J. Hanna, the CIM superintendent in Anhwei, on Thursday, December 13th. The magistrate in Wuhu told him that the bodies of the two missionaries had been found in Miaosheo.

John and Betty's parents were immediately informed by telegram, with deep condolences from the Mission's

To Die is Gain

representatives. Peter Stam wrote a letter to convey the news to wider family, friends and supporters.

> *Our dear children, John C. Stam and Elisabeth Scott Stam, have gone to be with the Lord. They loved Him, they served Him, and now they are with Him. What could be more glorious? It is true, the manner in which they were sent out of this world was a shock to us all, but whatever of suffering they may have endured is now past, and they are both infinitely blessed with the joys of Heaven.*
>
> *As for those of us who have been left behind, we were once more reminded of our sacred vows by a telegram received from one of John's schoolmates in the Midwest – "Remember, you gave John to God, not to China." Our hearts, though bowed for a little while with sadness, answered, "Amen!" It was our desire that he, as well as we, should serve the Lord, and if that could be better done by death than by life, we would have it so. The sacrifice may seem great now, but no sacrifice is too great to make for Him Who gave Himself for us.*
>
> *We are earnestly praying that it will all be for God's glory and the salvation of souls. How glad we shall be if through this dreadful experience many souls shall be won for the Lord Jesus! How glad shall we be if many dear Christian young people shall be inspired to give themselves to the Lord as never before, for a life of sacrifice and service!*
>
> *We were honored by having sons and daughters minister for our Lord among the heathen, but we are more signally honored that two of them have won the martyr's crown. We are sure that our dear brother and sister, Dr. and Mrs. Charles E. Scott, both join us in*

> *saying, "The Lord gave, and the Lord hath taken away; blessed be the name of the Lord (Job 1:21 KJV)*[1]

Betty's parents did indeed share the Stams' continued faith in God's goodness, as well as their deep sense of personal loss. For theirs was an eternal perspective. In this present life, John and Betty had given, and lost, everything; but their parents' hope, as with theirs, was in the life to come. They trusted that God would continue to work out His purposes through John and Betty's deaths, just as He had through their lives. They took every opportunity to speak of God's faithfulness and give Him the glory, even in their sorrow.

Two days after hearing the news, Clara Scott wrote to friends:

> *We have been thankful that from the first we committed our three precious ones into the Lord's hands, and have prayed that His name might be glorified and His will done. We have, of course, prayed that, if it be in accordance with His plans for them, their lives might be spared to witness to His great power to release from physical danger. But at the same time we, if His name could be the more glorified through the sacrifice of their young lives, were still willing to give up our treasure into His hands, knowing that He would not carry out such a purpose unless the greater glory would result through their death than through their living witness.*
>
> *When the telegram came Thursday evening saying that Betty and John were with the Lord we did not mourn as*

---

1. Ibid, p. 200.

To Die is Gain

> *those who have no hope, but could not but feel that a great blessing might come to the cause of Christ here in China and also wherever their martyrdom might be known. We cannot but rejoice that they have been accounted worthy to suffer for His sake, and we cannot be sorry for them that thus early they have been released from all earthly trials and have entered into the glory provided for those who belong wholly to Him.*
>
> *They are not the ones to have sought release from working longer in this world of darkness, but the Lord must have been satisfied that their work here was completed, and that their willingness to die for Him will bring in a larger harvest of souls than as if they have lived many years longer. It has been brought to our hearts by many Chinese and foreign friends that the kernel of wheat that dies will bear much fruit — that it cannot fall to the ground in vain, and that two kernels will bear more fruit than one.*[2]

Both sets of parents received hundreds of letters and telegrams of condolences from all over the world. Several memorial services were held in both China and the United States to give thanks for John and Betty and to remember their sacrifice. Charles and Clara Scott held a "Triumph" service at their home in Tsinan, where John and Betty had been married less than eighteen months before. A large memorial service was also held at the "Star of Hope" mission in Paterson, New Jersey, where John had learned so much of ministry, and was remembered with great fondness. The auditorium, which seated 600, was soon filled to overflowing, and a loudspeaker was set

---

2. Ibid, p. 201.

John & Betty Stam

up at the church opposite the mission to accommodate all who wanted to pay their respects.

The hopes and prayers of many were that John and Betty's deaths would serve as a powerful witness to the truth of the gospel; a truth so precious that these young missionaries had been willing to give their lives for it. These prayers were answered. At the end of the memorial service held at the Moody Bible Institute, where John and Betty had met, around seven hundred students stood on their feet to demonstrate their willingness to give their lives to missionary service, wherever the Lord might send them. At Wheaton College, another two hundred students did the same.

Thousands of believers across the world testified to a renewed commitment to serving Christ, through the inspiration of John and Betty and their devotion to Him, even to death. The shocking event was also reported in newspapers across the world, so that millions of unbelievers heard of John and Betty's courage. It presented a powerful testimony, and some are known to have come to Christ through it.

Family members and friends of the Stams, even those already committed to Christian service, found their hearts deeply challenged by their example. Betty's brother Francis, studying at Princeton seminary at the time, wrote to his parents:

> *I know, if your experience has been at all like mine, that this wicked deed has jolted us powerfully out of the spiritual lethargy into which we had slipped, and that even though*

To Die is Gain

> *we thought we were giving our best, it wasn't enough and lacked the depth of consecration and the power of witness that we ought to have as God's ambassadors to men.*[3]

It also increased people's awareness of the political situation in China, and the great spiritual need there. Betty's sister Helen, who with her husband Gordon was still awaiting a decision from their Mission board about where they would be sent, testified that "this brutal slaying only intensified our convictions. Our desire to be sent to China then became so strong as to be painful. Every other consideration became secondary, for never did a country present itself in a needier light, and never could witness be made in a more strategic place than in China now, as she stands at the parting of the ways."[4]

At Wilson College, where Betty had studied for her first degree, a particular concern was felt for baby Helen Stam. The governing board there voted to "adopt" her as "The College Baby", and pledged that the entire cost of her higher education there, when the time came, would be covered by the college. The students at Wilson, and many others, sent monetary gifts to China to contribute to Helen's immediate needs. She had become known around the world as "The Miracle Baby." There were many offers from couples volunteering to adopt her, but Charles and Clara Scott wished to take that responsibility on themselves. Her survival was a cause of great joy and comfort to them. Clara Scott had written:

---

3. Ibid, p. 204.
4. Ibid, p. 204.

> *To me it is nothing less than a miracle that Baby Helen Priscilla has been spared. My husband said this morning, "All the hordes of wicked Communists couldn't harm that helpless babe, if it were the Lord's purpose to have her live to glorify His name and show His power."*[5]

John and Betty Stam were the 73rd and 74th martyrs of the China Inland Mission. The February 1935 edition of their monthly magazine, "China's Millions", contained an extended tribute to the couple, which ended with these words:

> *"It has been a long time since any event connected with the mission fields has made so wide and profound an impression in this country. We believe that John and Betty Stam may by their death have spoken even more loudly than by their brief lives of devoted service. Let no one call this ending of their earthly career a tragedy, for in reality it is a triumph."*[6]

In the decades since John and Betty Stam were killed, their courage has continued to inspire new generations of believers. Their example is powerful; the example of their conduct and their character, their wholehearted devotion to Christ, and their commitment to follow Him even to death. Yet even as we honor their sacrifice, we must remember the far greater one that inspired their obedience. John and Betty were willing to give up their lives because they followed the pattern of the Savior who laid down His life for them.

---

5. Ibid, p. 201.
6. Ibid, p. 206.

To Die is Gain

"This is how we know what love is: Jesus Christ laid down his life for us. And we ought to lay down our lives for our brothers and sisters" (1 John 3:16).

Fact File: China and the China Inland Mission

Before the Lord Jesus Christ ascended into heaven, He gave His disciples a job to do. In words that have become known as "The Great Commission", He told them to "go and make disciples of all nations, baptizing them in the name of the Father and of the Son and of the Holy Spirit, and teaching them to obey everything I have commanded you" (Matthew 28:19-20).

The book of Acts in the New Testament tells the story of how Jesus' disciples, empowered by the Holy Spirit, began to do just that. The good news of the gospel began to spread immediately through the witness of the early church, so that by the end of the first century A.D. it had begun to spread around the shores of the Mediterranean Sea, even reaching the remote island of Britain. The power and influence of the Roman Empire greatly contributed to this, as once Christianity became known in Rome its message could spread quickly to the many Roman colonies in conquered lands as far as Western Europe and North Africa.

To Die is Gain

However, it was much longer before the message of the gospel reached China, which may be partly explained by the poor links that existed between China and the West.

Historically, China had been a very isolated nation. One of the earliest civilizations developed there was on the fertile land around the Yellow River (or the Huang He). Although the river provided rich soil for crops, it could also be a formidable enemy. Over time, Chinese farmers learned how to use the river to their advantage in agriculture, devising irrigation systems to drain away the excess water and benefit their crops. As society advanced, China was ruled by a series of dynasties, ruling families who passed power down from generation to generation. There were periods of great invention and advance, particularly in the fields of science and technology. One invention that attracted the interest of traders all over the world was silk. The Chinese were the first to discover the process by which raw silk from cocoons could be spun and woven into lengths of delicate material; and this was a product that immediately became very desirable, inspiring merchants from the West to undertake the long, dangerous journey to China in order to obtain it.

China was separated from even its nearest neighbors by some formidable barriers. Some of these were natural, geographical barriers; the Himalayan mountain range that divided it from India, the vast deserts to the north and west. But on top of this was added the man-

John & Betty Stam

made barrier of the Great Wall of China, constructed in the 3rd century B.C., which stretched for over fourteen hundred miles. Built into the enormous wall at regular intervals were turrets, which could serve as outposts for sentries and border guards, increasing the protection and isolation of the people within. It would be many centuries before stronger relationships between China and the rest of the world would be established, and that usually for the purpose of trade. Meanwhile, ignorance led to many rumors and misconceptions about the Chinese and their way of life.

There is evidence that some form of Christian teaching appeared in China as early as the 7th century under the Tang dynasty, but it did not take root until Jesuit missionaries reintroduced it during the 16th century. The first known Protestant missionary, Robert Morrison, arrived in China in 1807. Morrison, an Englishman, was the first to translate the Bible into Chinese. However, the ruling powers in China were extremely hostile towards Christian teaching, and missionary activity was officially prohibited. In spite of this, Western missionaries continued to spread the Christian message throughout the coastal regions of China that were open to foreign trade. They also made efforts to improve living conditions for the Chinese people by establishing schools, clinics and hospitals, distributing literature and arguing for social reforms, including the abolition of foot binding, better treatment of the serving classes and care of the poor.

Fact File: Hudson Taylor and the China Inland Mission

James Hudson Taylor was born in 1832, into a family of Christian believers in Barnsley, Yorkshire. His great grandfather, James Taylor, had been converted through the preaching of John Wesley, the Methodist preacher, who had visited the area in the early 1770s. Young Hudson rebelled against his parents' Christian faith for a time, but gave his own life to Christ at the age of seventeen. He committed his life to missionary work in China very soon afterwards, writing to his sister: "That land is ever in my thoughts. Think of it – three hundred and sixty million souls, without God or hope in the world! Think of more than twelve million of our fellowmen dying every year without any consolation of the Gospel – and scarcely anyone cares about it."[1]

Hudson studied medicine to equip him for missionary service and finally set sail for China in 1854, aged twenty-two. Originally he went out under the oversight of the Chinese Evangelization Society, but in

---

1. Kathleen White, *John and Betty Stam* (Bethany House Publishers, 1989), p. 18.

To Die is Gain

1865 he founded the China Inland Mission, with the vision of bringing the gospel to the whole of inland China. Taylor had worked hard to raise awareness of the spiritual need in China during his furlough, travelling extensively to churches around the United Kingdom. Within a year the new mission had managed to raise considerable funds and had twenty-one missionaries serving with them.

During the late nineteenth century many more missionaries were inspired to go out with the China Inland Mission, which had become well known around the world. Among these were "the Cambridge Seven"; seven educated, wealthy young men from Cambridge University, who chose to turn their backs on all the opportunities for advancement the world could offer them, in order to serve Christ in China. Such a remarkable choice aroused huge public interest.

Hudson Taylor had captured many hearts with his vision, and his missionaries earned a noble reputation. One writer observed: "They have an excellent spirit, – self-denying, with singleness of aim; devotional, with a spirit of faith, of love, of humility."[2] However, in 1899–1901 severe persecution broke out against them during what has become known as the Boxer Rebellion. The Boxers were a group of Chinese rebels who sought to "purify China of foreign oppression", particularly targeting Christian missionaries. More

---

2. Richard Lovett, *The History of The London Missionary Society 1795–1895* (London: Henry Frowde, 1899), p. 74.

than 70 CIM missionaries were killed. Shortly after this period of violence had come to an end, Dixon Hoste, one of the Cambridge Seven, took over as director of the mission. Hudson Taylor died in 1905 after many years of fruitful service. He has been and remains an inspiration to thousands.

Fact File: Communism in China

By the time John and Betty Stam went out to China, a new threat to missionary endeavour had arisen in the form of Communism. In the belief that everyone is equal, Communists seek to establish a society in which there are no distinctions between people in terms of social class or wealth. Rather, all property and means of production are divided equally. Even though the idea at the heart of this ideology sounds positive, attempting to create a Communist state has been fraught with problems. In places where communist philosophy has been adopted, it has quickly led to the loss of personal freedom and individuality. Ideas and independent thinking have been regarded with suspicion and seen as a threat to authority, and so religion of any kind is usually discouraged, unless it can somehow be carefully controlled by the Communist state. It is no surprise then, that Christian missionaries like the Stams found themselves in a dangerous position.

Although John and Betty were killed in 1934, it wasn't until 1949 that the Communist leader Mao

To Die is Gain

Zedong founded the People's Republic of China, after the Communists decisively defeated the Nationalists in a civil war. Many missionary organizations were forced to pull out of China at that point. The China Inland Mission tried to continue its work there, even bringing forty-nine new missionaries to Shanghai during 1948–1949. However, by 1950 it was decided that the continued presence of foreign missionaries was making life even more dangerous for the native believers, and reluctantly the CIM withdrew.

The mission established new headquarters in Singapore, seeking to reach out to people all over East Asia with the gospel. In 1964 it was renamed the Overseas Missionary Fellowship (OMF), which became OMF International in 1993. This extract from their website describes the situation today.

> *The nations of East Asia are still teeming with thousands who need to receive those "glad tidings" that Hudson Taylor sought to bring to the furthest points of China, and God is still leading. OMF International currently has nearly 3,000 staff, field workers and committed volunteers from 30 nations—1,400 of those are workers reaching out in East Asia.*

By the grace of God, the Communists did not manage to stamp out Christianity in China. Today, China officially remains an atheist country, but it is estimated that there are 97.2 million Christians living there. Despite the prohibition of religion, and despite periods of intense persecution, it is believed that there are more Christian believers in China today than there are members of the Communist Party.

However, China still needs our prayers. Christians are very much a minority group, making up less than seven percent of the total population. The Communist state still seeks to control all religious activity, and those under eighteen are banned from attending church. Churches are monitored and often attacked, and church leaders can face imprisonment. Those converting from other faiths, such as Islam or Buddhism, are at risk of being rejected or even attacked within their communities and often choose to keep their faith a secret.

You can find out more at www.operationworld.org and www.opendoorsuk.org.

John and Betty Stam: Timeline

1865	The China Inland Mission founded by Hudson Taylor.
1900	The Boxer Rebellion. Many foreigners and missionaries are driven out of the country.
1906	Elisabeth Alden Scott born in Albion, Michigan. Six months later the family sail to China, to serve as missionaries in the northern province of Shantung.
1907	John Cornelius Stam born in Paterson, New Jersey.
1921	The Communist Party of China is established.
1922	John Stam gives his life to Christ.
1924	Betty Scott moves to the U.S. to study at Wilson College in Chambersburg, Pennsylvania.
1925	Betty attends the "Keswick" Convention in New Jersey.
1929	John resigns from his office job to pursue full time Christian ministry.
1929	John and Betty meet while studying at the Moody Bible Institute in Chicago, in a prayer group for the China Inland Mission.
1931	John serves as an interim pastor in Elida, Ohio.
1931	Betty sails for China to serve as a missionary with the CIM.
1932	John sails for China, also with the CIM. John and Betty are reunited in Shanghai and become engaged.

1933	John and Betty get married at the Scotts' home in Tsinan. After their honeymoon, they return to Suancheng.
1934	John and Betty celebrate the birth of their daughter, Helen Priscilla Stam. Two months later, they move to Tsingteh, in the Anhwei province.
December 1934	John and Betty Stam are arrested by the Communist soldiers, and executed on 6th December. Three-month-old Helen Stam is rescued and taken to safety.

Thinking Further Topics

The Day the Soldiers Came
How did John and Betty respond to the rumors, and then the reality of the Communist invasion?
What do you think shaped their response?

A Voyage of Discovery
What was it that changed Peter Stam's outlook on life?
How did his faith in Christ go on to affect his choices and his lifestyle?
If you are a Christian, how does your faith impact your life?

An Independent Spirit
What do you think held John back from becoming a Christian earlier?
What lessons did he learn as he began to follow Jesus?
Can you identify with any of his struggles?

Living by Faith
How did John's faith in God grow during his years at college?
What did other people think of him?

Missionary Child
How were Betty Scott and her siblings influenced by their parents' example?

Standing on the Rock
How did Betty's childhood faith mature through her illness and her college years?
What was it about Betty that attracted other people?
Think about the qualities you most admire in other people. Are they similar to the qualities Betty showed, or are they more influenced by the world's values?

Testing the Waters
Why did John and Betty want to take things slowly in their relationship?
Who came first?
Think about the things that are most important to you in life. Is God at the top of the list, or is He competing with something or someone else?

Go Forward!
Why do you think John was chosen to address his class at their graduation? How do you think his words would have inspired them?

To China at Last

The young men on the boat with John commented that the Christians "seemed so free." What do you think they meant?

In what sense are Christians free?

If you're not sure how to answer, rereading what John wrote in his journal might help.

How did God demonstrate His goodness to John and Betty?

Blessings and Trials

What were some of the blessings and trials that Betty experienced as she began her missionary service in Fowyang?

How did they affect her?

Learning the Language

What was John's attitude to discomforts?

Think about how you respond to difficulties in your life and whether John's example could encourage you. Complaining comes much more easily to most of us than thanksgiving, but God will gladly help us to change if we ask Him.

New Horizons

What challenges did John face during his first few months in Suancheng?

What do you think motivated him to keep going "out of his comfort zone"?

The New Mr. and Mrs. Stam
How did God bless John and Betty as they started their new life together?
Do you think marriage changed their priorities? If so, how?

Becoming Parents
God soon blessed John and Betty with a baby daughter. Do you think having a child affected their priorities? If so, how?

To Live is Christ ... to Die is Gain
Despite the terrifying ordeal they were going through, how did John's words and behavior show that he was still trusting in God?

A Miraculous Rescue
What made baby Helen's rescue so miraculous?
How do you think it would have been a comfort to John and Betty's families in their grief?

Triumph
How did the families of John and Betty respond to their horrific deaths? Do you find their response surprising?
How were others inspired by the example of John and Betty?
Why would anyone describe what happened to them as a "triumph"?

Betty's life verse was Philippians 1:21: "To live is Christ and to die is gain."

Take some time to think and pray about what you have learned through reading about the lives and deaths of John and Betty Stam.

CHRISTIAN FOCUS PUBLICATIONS

Christian Focus | Christian Heritage | CF4K | Mentor

Christian Focus Publications publishes books for adults and children under its four main imprints: Christian Focus, CF4K, Mentor and Christian Heritage. Our books reflect our conviction that God's Word is reliable and Jesus is the way to know him, and live for ever with him.

Our children's publication list includes a Sunday School curriculum that covers pre-school to early teens, and puzzle and activity books. We also publish personal and family devotional titles, biographies and inspirational stories that children will love.

If you are looking for quality Bible teaching for children then we have an excellent range of Bible stories and age-specific theological books.

From pre-school board books to teenage apologetics, we have it covered!

Find us at our web page:
www.christianfocus.com

CF4·K
Because you're never too young to know Jesus